Careers in Marketing:

The Comprehensive Guide to Traditional and Digital Marketing Careers

©2016 Eric Siebert

ISBN: 13:978-1522922643

ISBN: 10:1522922644

Printed by: CreateSpace

Author contact information:

Eric Siebert

96 Country Drive Weston, MA 02493

P9-DGS-854

CONTENTS

Introduction
About This Book
How This Book Is Organized

Part 1: Marketing Overview
    What Marketers Do
    The 4 Ps of Marketing
    Where Does Digital Fit into the 4 Ps?

Part 2: Marketing Careers
 Market and Customer Insights
    Market Research Management
    Related Careers
      Qualitative Research
      Quantitative Research
      Syndicated Research
      Focus Group Moderator
      User Experience Research
 Marketing Planning
    Brand Management
    Product Marketing
    Corporate Brand Management
    E-commerce Marketing
    Related Careers
      E-commerce Merchandising
      Direct Response Marketing

Marketing Execution

Overview: The Marketing Funnel
Advertising Management
Media Management
Consumer Promotion
Trade Marketing
Shopper Marketing
Event Marketing
Demand Generation Marketing
   Lead Generation
   Customer Relationship Marketing
Digital Marketing Communications
Search Engine Marketing
Website Communication
Social Media Management
   Social Media Manager
   Social Media Community Manager
Related Careers
Marketing Optimization
   Marketing Analytics
   Digital Marketing Analytics
   Related Careers

Part 3: The Industry View of Marketing

Part 4: Final Thoughts

Appendix 1: Great Marketing Companies to Begin Your Market Career With
Appendix 2: Marketing Resources
Appendix 3: Marketing Association Websites
Appendix 4: Marketing Job Websites

INTRODUCTION

It seems the term *marketing* is thrown about by everyone these days—from politicians (Is the candidate marketable?) to celebrities (The marketing of my personal brand) to entrepreneurs (How do I market this great new product?). However, what *marketing* actually means is never quite explained. Even those of us that work in the profession still struggle to answer the simple question: What do marketers do?

If you're reading this book, it's likely that you're trying to gain a clear understanding of the term and what it means from a career standpoint. I decided to write this book to provide exactly that—clarity about the profession of marketing and the key job opportunities in the field.

I have been advising on marketing careers for some time but noticed a pressing need when teaching digital marketing at Bentley University. My students were mostly majoring in marketing, all very bright and ready to begin their careers within a year or two. I devoted one lecture to careers in marketing. And while attendance of (and attention during) my usual lectures could be spotty, this session was a full house of students leaning in to learn more.

I think it's clear that neither business schools nor most marketing professionals do an adequate job of providing guidance on the vast array of marketing career tracks. Whether because of my talent or dumb luck, I have had the opportunity to work on the front lines of traditional as well as digital marketing across many industries, including consumer packaged goods, information technology, media and entertainment, consumer electronics, and health care. I have seen the slow decay of traditional marketing approaches and the rise of the data-driven digital age. I've seen marketing innovation brilliance and hair-brained schemes presented as "new business models." As the saying goes, "I've been around the block."

My goal is to provide you with honest, unbiased, and real insights into the good, bad, and ugly of specific career options to help you point your career compass as accurately as possible. This book provides a snapshot of the full landscape of marketing career options, focusing deeply on the client side of marketing careers, career options with the companies that make the products and services sold.

Truth be told, my goal after graduating from business school in 1983 was to land a job in advertising. I spent months sending hundreds (thousands?) of résumés to every ad agency I could find. Luckily, my only job offer at the time was on the client side. If I had had detailed understanding about the client side of marketing, it would have been obvious this was a far better career fit for me. So a book like this sure would have saved me a lot of time (and postage) back then.

I've been blessed to have learned from and worked with some of the smartest, nicest, and most professional marketers on the industry. My eternal gratitude to the following people: Debra Gish, Pete McGregor, Ed Tashjian, Helen Nichols, Tom Murano, Mike Bauer, Marianne Schoenauer, Cees Talma, David Stern,

Tony Romeo, Paul Banas, Warren Stoll, Mark Greatrex, Matt Shattock, Ben Arno, John Nugent, Scott Fichten, Ashley Swartz, Ben Arno, Seth Solomons, Gregory Lee, Sue Shim, Unsoo Kim, Chonhong Ng, Tony Kim, Sunmi Kim, Maureen McGuire, Jared Cohen, Mike O'Conner, Mary Beth Moynihan, Dave Bierut, Harry Grey, Gevry Fontaine, Lia Aran, and Jackie LaFuente.

I would also like to thank the talented people that greatly assisted my with this book including my copyeditor Wendell Anderson and book cover designer Vanessa Mendozzi.

This book is dedicated to my wife Karen, daughter Julia and son Jeremy who gave me their love and inspiration to complete this work.

ABOUT THIS BOOK

If you're considering a career in marketing but can't answer the question what do marketers do, you are not alone. And when you don't have a clear grasp of what marketers do, it's kind of tough to understand what career options are available. And when you don't know what options are available, it's impossible to narrow in on the right career path for you.

I wrote this book to bring all of this into focus. My goal is to help you, the reader, take control of your marketing career by providing a comprehensive and unbiased guide to career options, and to help you decide which best suit your passions, capabilities, and aspirations.

If this supports some people in making smarter life decisions, it will have been well worth the time I have put into this writing.

BOOK ORGANIZATION

This book organizes career opportunities according to the four main activities of marketing presented in sequential order:

1. Customer and market insights
2. Marketing planning
3. Marketing execution
4. Marketing optimization

Customer and market insights are at the core of all marketing activities. This career path is about capturing and interpreting customer and market knowledge that guides all areas of the marketing mix. This section describes the client-side market research career in detail and provides a synopsis of related careers, including syndicated, quantitative, and qualitative research analysts, and focus group moderator.

Marketing planning is responsible for developing the overall business plan for a product or service and determining all elements of the marketing mix, including product development, pricing, distribution, and promotion. At the heart of marketing planning is the customer value proposition that articulates what the product being sold truly offers the customer and why it should be chosen over other alternatives in the market. This section reviews career options involving the planning and overseeing of all or most components of the marketing mix. Detailed descriptions of brand management, product management, e-commerce, and corporate brand management are provided, along with a synopsis of direct marketing and e-commerce merchandising roles.

The **marketing execution** section explains career options that bring the marketing strategy to life by creating and implementing all components of the marketing mix. We review in detail career options in client-side advertising, demand generation, consumer and trade promotion, shopper marketing, and event marketing, as well as opportunities within digital marketing, website communication, social media, and search marketing. A brief summary of related roles—such as content marketing, interaction and user experience, design, and the core areas of web development—are also provided.

Marketing optimization focuses on analyzing data to maximize the return on investment of marketing campaigns. This section provides not only a description of marketing analytics and digital marketing analytics but also a brief explanation of social media analytics, web analytics, and marketing operations roles.

Each section begins with a brief explanation of key responsibilities within the marketing activity and why they matter. This is followed by a summary of the most common (or emerging) career options and key information including:

- Typical job descriptions: along with my opinionated commentary about what the job description really means
- Success criteria: detailing the skills and competencies critical for success
- A day in the life: providing some context to a typical working day for select careers
- Pros and cons: the good and bad things to consider for each career track

- Career path: which career path (if any) the position might provide
- Salary guidance: a rather unreliable guesstimate based on a recent job board data
- Landing your first job: providing suggestions to break into the field

Traditional versus Digital Marketing

Certain marketing roles cannot be neatly divided into solely traditional or digital ones since most include some digital or technological component. Traditional marketing careers will mean those not currently dominated by digital, whereas careers in digital marketing will mean those roles that exclusively focus within digital media and related technologies. Special focus is placed on digital marketing execution roles, including digital marketing management, search marketing, web communication management, social media, and community management.

Client Side versus Agency and Consultant Roles

Marketing activities are performed by three key players: the client and the agencies and specialized consultants who support them. This book focuses primarily on career options commonly available on the client side, that is, the companies that manufacture the product or provide the service purchased by the customer. Also note that sometimes the term *consumer* is used and other times *customer*. While, there are some convoluted explanations of the differences between these terms, this book refers to the buyers of B2C (business to consumer) products as consumers and the buyers of B2B (business to business) products as customers.

The book concludes with some brief observations of careers through an industry lens, as well as final words of wisdom from yours truly. Lastly, the Appendixes provide additional information and resources to support your career search.

PART 1
MARKETING OVERVIEW

There are dozens of definitions of marketing, and if you read them all, you'd still struggle to gain clarity. Part of the problem is that marketers (myself included) like to make things much more complicated than they really are. (Job security I guess.) But it's also because the term *marketing*, like the term *business*, covers such a wide swath of activities. The following will hopefully add a bit more clarity.

In its broadest sense, marketing is a systematic approach to identifying, designing, and selling things that the customer finds of value. *Value* means the benefit received by the consumer in terms of functional benefits (for example, a faster laptop, a higher resolution TV), as well as emotional benefits (for example, the status achieved by wearing the latest fashion or the sense of security received by having the safest tires). The profession of marketing is about uncovering these tangible and intangible needs of consumers and delivering them to the market—for a profit.

What Marketers Do

Marketing is about the sequential planning and implementation of four main activities:
1. Customer and market insights
2. Marketing planning
3. Marketing execution

4. Marketing optimization

INSIGHTS   PLANNING   EXECUTION   OPTIMIZATION

Customer and market insights are used by marketers to predict the direction of an industry or product category and sense the needs of consumers. All great marketing programs result from superior customer and market insights. Anyone can manufacture a product but will it truly connect with the consumer and provide her something uniquely valuable? Or will it be simply be the same as other products and take its place in the discount bin?

Marketing success is grounded in knowing things your competition does not. This begins with an intimate understanding of the consumer—her unspoken needs, expectations, aspirations, and fears. A variety of research techniques is used to tease out this knowledge. It's painstaking work, but world-class marketing is not possible without world-class insights.

Marketing planning applies customer and market insights to identify new or enhanced products and services that better meet customer needs and then determines all elements of the marketing mix (the 4 Ps of marketing: Product, Price, Place, Promotion) to deliver this.

The 4 Ps of Marketing

Product: It's obvious that the marketer must determine what product to produce. But what's not obvious is identifying a product that brings something uniquely of value to the marketplace, the better mousetrap. All good product development begins with identifying a unique feature or benefit that's currently not available to the consumer. With this in hand, the marketer works side by side with research and development and packaging design and engineering teams to perfect all aspects of the product.

Price: The marketer also decides at what price to sell the product. Price the product too high and sales volume will be hurt; price it too low and profitability will suffer. This means finding that perfect price point that maximizes overall sales and profitability.

Place: Once the product is made, the marketer has to deliver it to the end user —at what 'place' will the consumer actually buy it? There are many different options available to the marketer, including selling it directly to the end customer, using a variety of third parties such as retailers to distribute it, or a combination of these. This distribution decision profoundly impacts all aspects of the marketing plan.

Promotion: With the product produced and distributed to the market, the marketer must create a plan to stimulate consumer demand largely through advertising and promotional activities that encourage product trial or repeat purchase. The options available to the marketer to do this are limitless, however, marketing budgets are not. The marketer is perpetually on a quest to find the perfect mix or promotional programs that maximize sales and profitability within the available budget.

The marketer will write the marketing strategy providing a detailed recommendation of the strategy, tactics, and investment for each of these 4 Ps. Of course, this investment comes with a commitment by the marketer to achieve specific annual sales, profit, and market share objectives. It is the combination of the marketing strategy and objectives that form the annual business plan that is the core responsibility of the marketer to deliver.

Marketing execution plans and creates the many specialized activities required to bring the product to market, influence consumer brand perceptions, and motivate consumers to buy. This includes all forms of marketing communication such as advertising, digital, social media, point-of-sale marketing, consumer promotion, and trade marketing. Each of these areas requires a great deal of skill and expertise by a wide array of professionals.

Marketing optimization is responsible for measuring, analyzing, and continually improving the performance of market campaigns. The relentless optimization of a brand's advertising, event, promotional, and digital program performance is crucial to drive maximum effectiveness and efficiency of the marketing investment. The superior application and interpretation of data is the foundation of this important activity.

Where Does Digital Fit into the 4 Ps?

It should be no surprise that digital tools and technologies have radically altered the marketing universe. But the fundamentals of marketing do indeed remain the same. It's just that the opportunities within have exploded.

Digital technology can provide entirely new product development opportunities enabling a product to also become a service (for example, Nike Fuel band). Of course, e-commerce has created a global marketplace and profoundly altered where and how consumers buy products. And digital media and technologies have transformed the field of marketing communication.

Digital has indeed reinvented marketing but has not changed its core concept: create and market products of value to customers for a profit.

PART 2
MARKETING CAREERS

MARKET AND CUSTOMER INSIGHTS

The essence of business advantage is possessing knowledge your competition does not. Customer and market insights are the tools used by marketers to acquire this knowledge and guide them to make smarter and more informed business decisions.

Customer insights aid the marketer in identifying new product innovations. It helps him know which product formulations and packaging designs consumers prefer. It assists him in uncovering the secrets of shopping and why people buy what they buy. Customer insights also enable the marketer to find sharper ways to advertise and position the brand so it stands out in a crowded marketplace. Also, market insights guide the marketer to understand how his industry will be impacted by cultural, societal, and technological shifts and thus to make smarter future investment decisions.

As you might expect, the digital age has completely revolutionized this field. The volume and variety of digital and social data available has grown exponentially over the last 10 years, providing an unprecedented look into the customer's mind and her shopping habits. Advancements in computing technology (think IBM, Watson) have also made it possible to analyze mind-boggling volumes of data. But marketers still struggle to capture and apply these data to benefit their business.

This is a fascinating field that employs a variety of methods to gain unique and forward-looking views of the market, consumers, and marketing-campaign performance. For those of you with strong quantitative skills and an insatiable desire to get inside the head of the customer, this is a great career option with serious demand and growth potential.

> Great (or terrible) market research management is the indispensable rudder that points the marketing ship in the right direction.

Market Research Manager

(Also Called Customer Insights, Market Research Analyst)
The market research manager guides the brand or product manager across all elements of the marketing mix. She plans and executes research to answer the brand's most important questions:

- Who are our customers and what do they need?
- How can we develop products that provide greater value to the customer?
- How should our products be designed or formulated to meet customer needs?
- Should we invest (millions) in advertising campaign option A or B?
- Where is the market going? What will it look like in 5 years? In 10 years?

- How do customers view our brand versus that of the competition?
- How is the market segmented, and which customer segments offer the most business potential?

Where and how to look for these answers is the core function of the market research manager.

- What research techniques should be used?
- What customer sample size and profiles are appropriate?
- Should the research be qualitative or quantitative?
- Do digital and social channels provide any unique insights into the customer?

The market research manager first develops the research brief documenting all key information guiding the research: objectives, profile of the type of consumer to be researched, how many of them (sample size), timing, and budget. She then decides the type of research that best answers the questions at hand:

- Should the research be qualitative (direct feedback from customers via focus groups or one-on-one interviews) or quantitative (via surveys)?
- What tools and materials are required (questionnaires, discussion guides) to field the research?
- Which third-party market research vendors should be hired to conduct the research?

> As the saying goes, "Garbage in = garbage out." A focus group of consumers that doesn't match the profile of the target audience, or a

> poorly designed questionnaire, wastes time and money and could point the brand in the completely wrong direction. So pristine execution of the research is an incredibly important responsibility of the market research manager.

The market research manager then organizes the fielding of the study and oversees its implementation. She then collects the research data, ensures its validity, and analyzes it. Finally she writes and presents her conclusions about what the research has revealed and recommends what the brand or company should do about it.

- Is the new product idea a hit or a miss?
- What new market trends are ripe for innovation?
- Is anyone able to recall the important messages in the ad campaign?

The work of the market research manager does indeed have a huge influence on the company's future direction.

Typical Job Description: Market Research Manager

Formal Job Description	What This _REALLY_ Means
Develop the most appropriate research activities that deliver unique and relevant customer and market insights that drive	Your work is challenging and a critical driver of success to the business. Your people will be relying on you to enlighten them.

competitive advantage.	
Meet with internal clients to identify knowledge gaps and prioritize key business issues.	You will be an indispensable part of the brand or product marketing team and will need to fully understand their goals and priorities.
Assess and select the most appropriate methodologies and techniques to achieve the research objectives.	There are many alternatives to choose from in research: focus groups, one-on-one interviews, heuristic research, ethnographic research. Your job is to determine which are best for the job at hand.
Design quantitative research questionnaires and qualitative focus group moderator guides.	All research begins with a clear description of the questions that need answers to guide the marketer. This can lead to a disaster if they are poorly written.
Ensure third-party research suppliers deliver accurate, timely, and meaningful insights.	Independent contractors hired by you will do much of the grunt work. They must be managed very closely to ensure they deliver pristine data.
Lead insight generation to inform brand positioning, campaign development, and media.	The research plays a big role in driving advertising, promotion, pricing, and branding decisions. It's your job to stop a major ad campaign if it's a bad idea.

Analyze and interpret research data. Write research conclusions and present actionable recommendations to clients, including senior management.	Sometimes research is not always clear or conclusive. Ultimately, it is your job "to land the research plane" and clarify what the research revealed and what the company should do about it.
Use industry best practices to monitor industry, category, and competitive market dynamics.	In addition to the micro understanding of the customer, you will be expected to manage the macro view of the overall marketplace, including the overall size of the market, new trends, and the key activities of competitors.

What You Need to Be Successful

Superior = mastery / Strong = better than average / Solid = competitive

Skills Required

- Superior knowledge of market research models and methodologies, including qualitative, quantitative, ad-hoc, and syndicated research
- Superior analytical thinking
- Superior written and oral communication
- Strong project management

Competencies Required

- Superior passion for understanding consumers
- Strong ability to build collaborative relationships
- Strong influencing skills

- Strong ability to multitask and manage multiple priorities

Pros	Cons
👍 You can make a major impact on the business. 👍 A highly strategic role. 👍 Less stressful than many marketing jobs. 👍 Decent work/life balance (most of the time). 👍 You work with smart people within a variety of marketing roles. 👍 Excellent job security. 👍 Good pay.	👎 A somewhat behind-the-scenes role. 👎 Much narrower in scope compared to brand manager or product manager roles.

Career Path of a Market Research Manager

Market research management is a great career choice for the right individual. You'll work with smart people, be at the forefront of your industry, and have the opportunity to make a real impact on the brand or company. As discussed in the Marketing Strategy section, you won't be the lead actor in the play but rather a critical supporting actor. This role is just fine with many talented people, but others may find it too specialized.

You will probably start your career as a market research analyst, doing some serious number crunching and report writing. This will be a behind-the-scenes role but a terrific way to cut your teeth in the industry. This deep analytical experience will provide you with a rich foundation of knowledge enabling you to quickly become the go-to person for answers.

In a relatively short period (two to three years), you should rise to the market research manager position. Assume you will stay (and grow) in this role for 7 to 10 years moving across different brands and categories. The next step up the ladder would be market research director, essentially managing a group of market research managers and coordinating the big picture for market/customer insights for the company. This is a high-profile and high-pressure position. It is indeed senior management's expectation that the company wins over competitors by always being ahead of the market. Delivering these insights year in and year out is on the shoulder of the market research director.

Salaries

Market research managers can expect to earn $75k to $140k plus a 15% to 25% bonus at companies with $1 billion dollars or more in annual sales revenue.

A Day in the Life of The…. Market Research Manager

8:30: Present latest competitive activity data to marketing and R&D

10:30: Present brand positioning data at ad agency creative briefing meeting

> 12:00: Working lunch with this evening's focus group moderator
>
> 13:00: Review vendor proposals for ad copy testing program
>
> 15:00: Present social media listening report for brand manager
>
> 16:00: Review new website design and social media program results
>
> 16:00: Prepare for market trend presentation to the division president
>
> 17:30: Review division president presentation with marketing research director
>
> 18:00: Leave office to drive to evening consumer focus group

Landing Your First Job

Breaking into market research, as with most marketing jobs, requires some proof points. Securing an internship in market research or data analytics is the best place to start. Contact focus group or quantitative research companies in your area. They often need well-spoken and organized people to find consumers to participate in research and to help coordinate the fielding of their quantitative and qualitative research programs.

But any internship that involves analytical work can provide some level of experience. Data exist everywhere and thus the opportunity to analyze them. You could also volunteer to conduct research for a local business—assess its Facebook or Twitter conversation, analyze its sales data for trends, or observe the behavior of its customers at its store and consider what that means for the business. Write up your conclusions and present them. You've now created your first proof point!

Also use LinkedIn to contact market research managers and other marketers to provide your analysis of the category trends, their recent ad campaign, or your experience when shopping for their product. Based on your assessment, propose to them your thoughts on new product ideas, better ad copy, or a new packaging idea. They will be impressed with your thinking and proactiveness. Thinkers are in indeed in short supply.

In the Final Analysis

Insights create the spark that leads to all blockbuster innovations, great new ad campaigns, and killer promotions. Steve Jobs famously said it's not the consumers' job to know what they want. And The Grateful Dead sang, "Once in a while you get shown the light in the strangest of places if you look at it right." Finding this light is the magic of this career path.

Customer and market insights are the heart and soul of marketing, and managers can make a huge difference in the future of their company or brand. There are excellent long-term career prospects, and while the pay is on the higher end of the scale, the stress level is on the lower end.

See Appendix 1 for a list of great companies to begin your career with.

Related Careers in Customer and Market Insights

Market research managers rely on market research agencies to perform specialized roles. Following are some brief explanations of the most important ones.

Qualitative Research Analyst

Qualitative research is usually performed by a specialized market research agency or a consultant. The qualitative research analyst works face to face with consumers to gain a deep understanding of the question at hand: their shopping habits, their perceptions of the brand or the competitors, what they think of a new product idea. Qualitative research analysts design and field the research through various methods, such as focus groups, one-on-one interviews, and ethnographic research (live observations of consumers in their homes or in the store shopping). Digital tools, such as Skype, are being increasingly used for qualitative research as well.

The qualitative research analyst role generally includes the functions of the focus group moderator role described later. Consider the qualitative research analyst a one-stop shop for qualitative research.

Quantitative Research Analyst

When considering investing millions in a new product or advertising campaign, marketers can't simply rely on their own intuition or the feedback of just a handful of people in a focus group. Quantitative research is used to test marketing ideas with large and statistically significant samples of consumers to provide marketers with much greater confidence in their decisions.

The quantitative research analyst designs and implements this research via online, telephone, mail, and in-person surveys. He develops the sampling plan (who and how many should be included in the research) and prepares the questionnaire or other material for the research. The quantitative research analyst then organizes all fieldwork required to distribute and collect the surveys, interpret the results, and present the written findings to the client. As expected, this role requires strong quantitative and statistical skills. Equally important is the analyst's full understanding of the goals of the marketer and translating this into accurate and actionable feedback.

Syndicated Research Manager

Companies rely on many forms of information to guide their business decisions, including global economic data, consumer trends, and the size of markets. These are very extensive and complex reports that are usually far too expensive for any company to pay for on its own.

The syndicated research manager leads the collection, analysis, and reporting of insights from syndicated, or third-party, published sources. The manager works with the company sponsor to identify its market intelligence needs and to secure third-party data sources to answer these questions. Since huge investments are often made based on this intelligence, the quality and reliability of the data sources is critical. Thus the syndicated research manager must have deep research and analytical skills and be able to clearly articulate findings through written reports and in-person presentations.

Focus Group Moderator

A focus group is a form of qualitative research that provides marketers with directional feedback from consumers. It provides preliminary insights into their needs, habits, and attitudes, but it is not used to make final marketing decisions.

A small group of consumers is gathered around a table to discuss a handful of general questions on the mind of the marketer.

- How do they decide what they are going to make for dinner on any given night?
- Where do they gather their information when considering buying a new TV?
- What are their perceptions of brand A versus brand B?

Managing these groups is no easy task. It's the job of the focus group moderator to get a group of strangers to speak openly and freely—sometimes about very personal things, sometimes about very mundane things. All the while your client observes you through a one-way glass window!

A great focus group experience is when the all participants lean in and openly share their honest thoughts. A bad focus group experience is when a single participant with a dominant personality monopolizes the conversation while the others just sit back and agree. The focus group moderator's role is to get everyone to talk and to stay focused on the topic at hand. Afterward the moderator crystallizes the entire discussion— what did the group collectively think across the key research questions? The focus group moderator then presents these observations and conclusions to the client in writing. It takes an exceptionally talented person to do this job well.

User Experience Researcher

We all have experienced websites that just work right, those sites that seem to sense what we are looking for and how we look for it. With just two or three clicks, we land on exactly the right web page. Of course, we have all also experienced websites that are confusing and frustrating. Achieving the former and preventing the latter is the role of the user experience researcher.

The user experience researcher is responsible for designing and conducting research to optimize the navigation, design, layout, and functionality of web and mobile digital properties. The ultimate goal is to ensure that visitors find the information they are looking for in an easy, fast, and intuitive manner.

The best user experience research managers combine expert knowledge of digital technology with a deep understanding of how people interact with digital media. Usability research is the primary tool used and places actual consumers in front of a website (or website prototype). The manager directs them through a series of tasks to assess how easy it is to achieve the task. The manager also explores how consumers interact with site applications and other functionality.

- Was it difficult to navigate the site?
- Could consumers find the desired information once they navigated to the right page?
- Did the content meet their expectations once they landed on the right page?
- Was the shopping cart easy to use?
- Was it placed on the correct web page?
- Was it located on the right area of the page?

With this information, the user experience manager briefs all parties (marketer, information architect, UX designer) on areas requiring further optimization. This is a very skilled role and requires training and hands-on experience. As investment in digital media increases, so does market demand for this extremely valuable skill set.

MARKETING PLANNING

Every marketing manager dreads the question: So what exactly do you do? Since manufacturing makes the product and the sales team sells the product and the finance team takes care of accounting and the ad agency creates the ads—what exactly do they pay you to do?

Here's where a good analogy helps. If an orchestra conductor does not write the music and does not play any of the instruments, what exactly does he do? Clearly, his job is to select that music that will delight the audience and get the very best sound out of the individual instruments and musicians. The conductor brings this together to create something greater than the sum of the parts: a symphony that stirs the soul.

A brand or marketing manager does the same thing across all elements marketing value. She determines what new product will delight the consumer and how to get the best out of all her players—sales, R&D, market research, promotion, the ad agency—ultimately creating and executing a marketing program that stirs desire and opens the wallet of the consumer. This section describes of four of these roles:
1. Brand management
2. Product management
3. Direct marketing
4. E-commerce management

An additional strategic role, corporate brand management, is also reviewed.

BRAND MANAGEMENT

Branding a product with a design or symbol has been around forever, but the management discipline of brand management was developed by Procter & Gamble in the 1950s. This approach was a revolutionary business concept and created the template for the marketing function within all fast-moving consumer goods (FMCG) companies (think of such companies as Unilever and Nestlé) ever since.

Brand management is a simple yet powerful idea that places the brand manager at the heart of business planning and execution for a specific brand. With one eye on creating value for the customer and the other on delivering business results, brand management directs the 4 Ps of marketing:
1. Product (what to sell)
2. Place (where to sell it)
3. Price (at what price)
4. Promotion (how to stimulate purchase demand)

Central to the brand management role is creating and marketing products that better meet the needs of the consumer. This begins with a deep understanding of the consumer, the current market, and emerging trends. These insights are used to identify what new products or improvements to existing products can provide better value to the consumer over those currently available in the market. This strategy forms the basis of the business plan and all the 4 Ps activities that create and bring the product to market.

The digital age has not revolutionized the discipline of brand management, but it certainly has evolved it. In a bygone era, TV advertising and a coupon in the Sunday paper were all that were required for a brand to reach the consumer. Digital has completely altered the communication landscape. Every consumer goods marketing program now includes a robust mix of digital advertising, social media, mobile, and website communication.

Brand Manager

The brand manager is essentially the CEO of a specific brand. The brand manager creates the annual business plan, writes the marketing strategy, and has the great responsibility of "owning" the P&L (the profit-and-loss statement). The business plan proposes specific revenue, profit, and market share targets for the fiscal year. These annual goals are then broken down into monthly targets—an important task that sets the direction for sales quotas, the manufacturing schedule, and marketing spending.

At the heart of the business plan is the marketing strategy, which details the activities that will deliver the revenue and profit goals. The marketing plan addresses a number of the key questions including:
- What is the brand strategy and positioning to distinguish it in the market?
- What new products will be introduced? When? At what price?
- What ad campaigns will be developed?
- How much of the budget should be spent on media and which type?

- How much will be invested in consumer promotions? Trade promotion?
- What new distribution channels should be considered?
- What special pricing and deals should be implemented at the store shelf?

Once the plan is completed, the brand manager must sell his plan to senior management. These meetings can be brutally tough and require convincing the powers that be (including the finance director) to believe in the rationale behind the strategy and approve the requested marketing program funding.

With the business plan approved, the brand manager then leads other specialists inside and outside the company to execute it. The brand manager briefs the advertising agency and consumer promotion department about key business priorities, market share goals, and the available budget. The brand manager works with the trade promotion department to plan retail pricing and the promotional programs that will run throughout the year. The brand manager also directs the work of market research, R&D, and the packaging design teams to develop entirely new products or to improve existing ones.

Typical Job Description: Brand Manager

Formal Job Description	What This _REALLY_ Means
Lead development of the business plan for the brand establishing sales, market share, and profit objectives.	You are the chief executive offer of the brand and are running a company within a company.
Develop the marketing	You must see the big picture,

strategy that delivers the business plan objectives.	where the market is and where it is going. The pressure is on you to deliver a strategy that beats the competition and gets results.
Develop compelling and differentiating brand strategy and positioning.	People buy brands they connect with. You need to figure out how to unlock the heart and the mind of the customer to make this connection.
Lead the planning of all marketing communication, including advertising, digital, and social media.	You get to lead a lot of very smart, creative, passionate, and opinionated people. God help you!
Lead promotion planning, including the alignment of trade, shopper, and consumer promotions.	The ultimate battleground is the supermarket shelf. You will devote a lot of time to this area.
Develop the pricing strategy that maximizes sales velocity and gross profit.	If you price it too high, no one will buy it. If you price it too low, you won't make any profit. You need to figure out this moving target.
Lead new product development.	Companies innovate or they go out of business. Everyone will be looking to you to come up with the next great new product idea.
Guide market research to understand market trends and customer needs and	Your job is to ask the questions today that lead to the opportunities of tomorrow. Not

motivations.	many people know how to do this well. You must be one of them.

What You Need to Be Successful

Superior = mastery / Strong = better than average / Solid = competitive

Successful brand managers possess a solid combination of entrepreneurial, strategic thinking, leadership, and planning capabilities. It's truly a multidimensional role that wears many hats and interacts with everyone in the organization. The brand manager must be able to talk shop with the deep-thinking scientists in R&D. She needs to gain the trust and partnership of the hard-charging sales force and needs a creative eye to guide the work of the ad agency and promotion department. The superior brand manager works hard to earn the respect of all functions within the business.

Skills Required
- Superior strategic thinking
- Superior customer orientation
- Strong analytic thinking
- Superior project management
- Strong writing skills
- Superior verbal communication skills

Competencies Required
- Superior leadership skills
- Superior ability to motivate others
- Superior ability to build collaborative relationships
- Strong entrepreneurial drive
- Solid creative and conceptual thinking

Pros	Cons
👍 Exceptional business training.	👎 Typically involves marketing not-so-sexy household brands.
👍 Highly entrepreneurial.	👎 Very high stress level.
👍 Lots of responsibility at a young age.	👎 Can be long hours on a regular basis.
👍 The ability to run one's own business.	👎 Dominated by slow-growth industries.
👍 No two days are the same.	👎 Intense competition for promotions.
👍 The fastest route to executive management.	👎 Executive jobs are ultracompetitive.
👍 Combines business with creativity.	
👍 Work with variety of people and professions.	
👍 Very good compensation.	
👍 Rapid career advancement.	

Career Path of the Brand Manager

Your first job will be as an assistant brand manager (brand assistant), and you will be assigned to a specific brand, working directly for the brand manager. Training approaches vary significantly across companies, but you will likely be assigned primary responsibility for specialized tasks, such as managing the sales forecast, running the brand website, analyzing the market, or working on a consumer promotion program. Most important, you will gain exposure to all critical aspects of running the business, essentially trailing your brand manager to key strategic, advertising, sales, and other meetings. This exposure is critical to your professional development.

Your first promotion (within one to two years) is to associate brand manager level where you will get meatier responsibilities—perhaps leading the national consumer or trade promotion programs. Once you have proven proficiency across the 4 Ps, you'll earn your brand manager stripe (usually within three to five years). The next rung up the ladder is marketing director (7 to 10 years). This level is also called *group marketing manager* and *category manager* and is responsible for a portfolio of brands within a specific category (for instance, Nestlé's coffee brands). Vice president of marketing comes next (10 to 15+ years) and is responsible for all brands within a specific line of business, for example, all beverage or all snack brands within the company.

Brand management provides a strong avenue to the top of the ladder, CEO, within an FMCG company. Unlike other functions, such as finance and sales, the marketer will already have extensive experience in managing the dynamics of the consumer marketplace and the complexities of running all facets of the business. You have been preparing to run the company for your entire career!

Salaries
Salaries vary widely for brand manager depending on whether you have an MBA, the size of company, and location. Here is a rough guide to companies with $1 billion+in sales revenue:
- Assistant brand manager: $70k to $90k plus a 10% to 15% bonus

- Brand manager: $75k to $120k plus a 15% to 20% bonus
- Marketing director: $140k to $180k plus a 20% to 30% bonus
- Marketing VP: $180k to $280k plus a 30% to 50% bonus

A Day in the Life of the Brand Manager

8:00: Coffee with sales director to discuss sales forecast

8:30: Innovation planning meeting with R&D

10:00: Meet with ad agency to review TV ad storyboards and media plan

12:00: Lunch with brand manager colleagues

13:00: Weekly project status meeting with boss (marketing director)

14:00: Interview summer intern candidate

15:00: Review new website design and social media program results

16:00: Prepare for presentation of monthly results to division president

17:30 Review division president presentation with marketing director

18:00: Clean up e-mail inbox; return missed calls

Landing Your First Job

An entry-level job in brand management at a large company usually requires an MBA, typically from a top school. However, a BS/MS degree in marketing is sometimes acceptable if the candidate has solid work experience in a related area, such as advertising or promotion.

Even with an MBA, many companies still expect some marketing related experience—whether it is at small company or a summer internship. When interviewing, it is critical to highlight your entrepreneurial experiences and ambitions. Even if you haven't started your own business, bring a well thought through voice of the customer perspective. Go buy the company's products, spend some time using them, and consider how the marketing could be improved. Stand out in your interview by recommending enhancements to the company's advertising, digital strategy, or packaging design. It doesn't matter if your recommendations are right or wrong. You just want to show that you're a thinker who can create the future.

In the Final Analysis

Brand management provides unmatched business training and is the pathway to senior management at consumer goods companies. So if running a large business—with someone else's money—at a very young age sounds interesting, consider the career path of the brand manager.

See Appendix 1 for a list of great companies to begin your career with.

PRODUCT MARKETING

Product management generally describes marketing careers at companies that sell more complex products. These include business-to-business (B2B) and business-to-consumer (B2C) companies within high tech (information technology, consumer electronics, and telecommunications), financial services, health care, and other industries.

Product marketing usually focuses on just three of the 4 Ps of marketing: promotion, place, and pricing. Unlike brand management, this role has limited influence over product development and innovation. Also, the company's brand is managed by corporate marketing, which leads development of the brand strategy and positioning.

The terms *upstream marketing* and *downstream marketing* best illustrate the difference between brand management and product management.

Upstream marketing refers to the strategic planning activities that drive product innovation: market planning, R&D, and core technology investments. Within brand management, marketing fully leads upstream marketing. However, within large tech-driven companies, these decisions are led by engineering, R&D, and strategic planning. Product marketers are increasingly getting a seat at the upstream table, though, bringing fresh customer and market insights to the innovation process.

Downstream marketing activities are at the heart of product management focusing on pricing, advertising, channel management, and promotion for existing products while leading the successful commercialization of new product introductions.

Product Manager

The product manager is responsible for a single product line, for example, home printers, and leads marketing planning and execution for new and existing products. He works closely with sales to establish pricing and to expand distribution of the product into various distribution channels. He also leads the development of marketing communication and promotion programs, including trade shows, trade promotion, advertising, consumer promotion, and digital marketing programs.

Product managers primarily use the same type of advertising and promotional programs we reviewed in the brand management section. Traditional (TV, print, radio, outdoor) and digital advertising programs are developed by the product manager to create awareness and consideration for the product. Consumer and trade promotions (coupons, special offers) are developed to stimulate purchase and maintain customer loyalty. In B2B companies, product managers also lead demand-generation marketing activities to find and channel leads to the sales force and to maintain ongoing marketing communication with the customer to foster brand loyalty. (These activities, lead generation and customer relationship marketing, are described in detail in the Marketing Execution section.)

There is a huge opportunity to make a difference in this role, as evidenced by Samsung's Next Big Thing campaign. Here's where an excellent product was supported by a brilliant marketing campaign resulting in a home run success.

Typical Job Description: Product Manager

Formal Job Description	What This _REALLY_ Means
Manage the product marketing process from strategic planning to market execution.	You will be running a business - within – a - business. It's a big job that impacts and interacts with many people in the organization.
Plan and execute marketing programs to generate and nurture sales leads.	You'll be developing a variety of programs—such as trade shows, direct mail, digital marketing, and telesales—to find potential buyers and funnel these leads to the sales force.
Lead the new product launch-planning process across key functional teams, including R&D, engineering, and marketing communications.	Someone has to bring it all together and bring the product to market. That someone is you!
Lead planning for all marketing communication, including advertising, digital, and social media.	You will be deciding where to spend millions of dollars. You need your right brain to judge great creative

	work and your left brain to make sure the money is spent wisely.
Drive customer loyalty by building customer-relationship marketing programs.	You need to be well versed in the latest and greatest marketing automation technologies such as salesforce.com.
Maintain a leading-edge understanding of industry trends and customer buying dynamics.	You are expected to be the foremost expert in customer insights and need to be able to predict the future!
Develop the pricing strategy that maximizes sales velocity and gross profit.	If you price it too high, no one will buy it. If you price it too low, you won't make any profit. You need to figure it out.
Prepare marketing materials to support the sales force and key customer accounts.	There are some tedious and boring aspects to every job. But everything matters and must be done well.
Measure and report marketing-campaign performance metrics.	Your world: Plan — Execute —Measure- —Report— Optimize. REPEAT!

What You Need to Be Successful

Superior = mastery / Strong = much better than average / Solid = competitive

Superior product managers know their market and customers better than anyone else on the planet. They are leaders who motivate and mobilize sales, advertising, promotion, and others within the organization. Success is based on the depth of their strategy, their ability to effectively execute marketing programs, and to quickly course correct their program as market dynamics rapidly change.

Skills Required
- Superior strategic thinking
- Superior analytical thinking
- Strong strategic planning aptitude
- Strong quantitative aptitude
- Strong written and verbal communication skills
- Strong organizational skills

Competencies Required
- Superior ability to build collaborative relationships, especially with sales
- Strong customer orientation
- Strong ability to motivate others
- Strong leadership skills
- Strong teamwork skills
- Solid creative-thinking abilities

Pros	Cons
👍 You usually work in dynamic industries.	👎 You have limited responsibilities for new product development, although this is changing at some companies.
👍 You get lots of responsibility quickly.	
👍 No two days are the same.	
👍 Good career advancement potential.	👎 The jobs can be highly stressful.
👍 You can make a real difference to the success of your company.	👎 There are often long hours and frequent travel.
👍 You work with variety of people and professions.	👎 There is intense competition for promotions.
👍 The pay is generally very good.	👎 Rising to the executive ranks is ultracompetitive.

Career Path of a Product Manager

The career path of a product manager varies significantly from company to company. But you will likely begin as an assistant product manager and then progress to product manager then marketing director and finally to vice president of marketing. As you rise in the ranks, you will gain responsibility for an increasingly larger portfolio of products. When you achieve the role of director (seven to ten years), you will usually become responsible for managing not just products but also the category. Here you will need to make critical decisions about how to segment the category (for example, premium segment versus mainstream segment versus value segment) and what the best marketing strategy is to compete within each segment.

At the vice president of marketing level (15+ years), you will not only manage all products within your division but also have an important seat at the table in terms of defining next-generation innovations and appropriate acquisitions. Product management is indeed a route to senior management but not necessarily to CEO. Depending on the industry or company, other functions—such as sales, engineering, or finance—may be better positioned to get the top job.

Salaries

Product management salaries also vary widely, depending on the company. Here is a rough guide to companies with $1B+ revenue:

- Product manager: $80k to $120k plus a 15% to 20% bonus
- Marketing director: $140k to $180k plus a 20% to 30% bonus
- Marketing VP: $180k to $280k plus a 30% to 50% bonus

 A Day in the Life of the Product Manager

8:00: Prep for new product trade show with event team

8:30: Meet with a key customer about the comarketing program

10:00: Review price elasticity study

12:00: Update holiday sales forecast with sales director

13:00: Release to sales force the new dealer incentive program

> 14:00: Meet with digital marketing team to review website conversion results
>
> 15:00: Ad agency presents holiday blitz media plan proposal
>
> 16:00: Department meeting to review and discuss new competitive activity
>
> 17:30: Clean up e-mail inbox; return missed calls

Landing Your First Job

Entry-level product management jobs are possible but almost always require an MBA and some prior work (or internship) experience. But product managers most frequently come out of the sales, marketing communication, or even engineering departments.

If you have a passion for a particular industry, such as consumer electronics, assess any and all entry-level options. Especially consider entering within a sales role. Sales experience provides excellent industry training. And if you can then demonstrate a superior grasp of the market and your customers, you should be a prime candidate for a product manager role within two to three years.

While product management might be a challenging field to land your first job, more and more companies are addressing the need for strategic customer- and market-oriented talent. They also desperately need digitally savvy people to bring their marketing programs into the 21st century. So there is a lot of opportunity once you get your foot in the door.

In the Final Analysis

If want to work in a more dynamic industry than FMCG, product marketing offers robust opportunities to practice the profession of marketing. You'll have limited influence over the product innovation pipeline, but your pricing, channel-management, and demand-generation skills will pay you handsomely, and you will have solid long-term career prospects.

See Appendix 1 for a list of great companies to begin your career with.

CORPORATE BRAND MANAGEMENT

Large companies that sell many products under a single brand name—such as Sony, Fidelity, and GEICO—typically manage their brand within the corporate marketing department. The heart of this function is brand positioning, the art and science of establishing a distinctive 'position' in the mind of the customers. The goal is to find that position that clearly defines what the brand stands for, what value it provides, and why it should be chosen over competitive offerings. Once determined, the company will use this positioning to guide all of its marketing communications, such as advertising, packaging, and promotional material. Thus millions (often hundreds of millions) of dollars depend on the work of the corporate brand director.

> "Products are produced in factories, but brands are produced in the mind." Corporate brand management shapes how the brand is perceived by consumers and their understanding of why they should do business with you.

Nike, Apple, IBM, GE, and Coca-Cola are at the pinnacle of corporate brand management. This is no accident. Corporate brand management work includes both heavy-duty strategic planning and relentless execution to ensure the brand message is clearly and consistently delivered in a premium way. It's an important job that profoundly impacts shareholder value.

Corporate Brand Director

The corporate brand director leads planning and execution of the brand plan, which includes three fundamental elements:

1. The brand assessment
2. The brand strategy
3. The brand execution

The corporate brand director undertakes an assessment to understand how the brand is currently perceived in the marketplace. She works with the market research department to gain a detailed understanding of how customers feel about the brand, what it offers them, and how this contrasts with competitors' brands.

- What does the brand uniquely provide the customer?
- What is the personality of the brand?
- How is it different from competitors' brands?

With this knowledge, the corporate brand director now tackles brand strategy, the heart of which is the brand positioning. As detailed previously, positioning guides all company communications so that it works synergistically to create a distinct position in the customer's mind—one that is compelling and distinctive, and that ultimately influences customer preference.

Once the brand positioning has been determined, the director then works closely with the advertising, digital, and others across marketing communications to execute the corporate

brand communication program. Typically, the centerpiece of this is a global advertising campaign supplemented by various digital, public relations, and other communication efforts. The corporate brand director is also responsible for ensuring that the brand positioning and brand identity (the logo and other design elements) are applied accurately and consistently globally. No wonder the brand manager is often referred to as the "brand cop." Finally, the corporate brand director is responsible for measuring key indicators of brand equity including brand awareness, perceptions and loyalty.

Typical Job Description: Corporate Brand Director

Formal Job Description	What This *REALLY* Means
Develop the corporate brand strategy, including the brand positioning, corporate marketing communication program, and brand measurement plan.	There is big money riding on your strategy, and all the parts need to be expertly planned with quantifiable success metrics.
Direct the corporate research team to develop global brand insights utilizing syndicated research, qualitative research, and competitive assessments.	While others will actually "do the fishing" for insights, you need to pilot the boat and show them where to fish.
Develop a compelling and distinctive brand positioning that strongly positions the brand in the mind of customers.	This is why you are paid —to find the key to the heart (and wallet) of the consumer.
Direct planning and execution for external marketing communication. Direct the ad agency and other communication partners to create traditional and digital marketing	A lot of people are expecting your clear guidance on how to take the strategy and turn it into advertising, digital, and social media programs and

communication programs.	other activities. You will be very busy!
Develop detailed brand objectives and work with market research to implement the brand measurement plan.	You will need to set goals to assess if your strategy is working, measuring changes in brand awareness and perceptions.
Work closely with various divisions, regions, and internal functions, such as human relations and investor relations, to develop the brand image among business partners, prospective employees, and investors.	Brand perceptions matter not just to the customer but also to your current and future employees, the communities the company works in, investors, and other stakeholders. You have a lot of people to think about!
Establish a global brand initiative to maintain a premium and consistent brand image globally.	As the "brand cop," your job is to maniacally protect the brand's image.

What You Need to Be Successful

Superior = mastery / Strong = much better than average / Solid = competitive

A position in corporate brand strategy requires significant experience received at an ad agency, brand consultancy, or on the client side as a brand manager.

You will need to have an insatiable thirst for learning about the customer—her needs (fears?) and how this forms her relationship with your brand. You will need to be able to take a 100-page research report and crystallize it into a handful of key insights that form the basis of the strategy. You will then need to clearly communicate the strategy to senior executives and others within your company—perhaps the toughest part of the job.

As with other marketing roles, you will need to partner with many people, both inside and outside of your company. Again, success will be based on the depth of your strategy and your ability to effectively direct the ad agency, marketing communications, and others to execute your program. It will also be important to show measurable results (via market research surveys) in growing brand awareness and positive brand perceptions.

Skills Required
- Superior customer orientation
- Superior written and verbal communication
- Strong organizational skills
- Strong strategic planning aptitude
- Solid analytical thinking
- Superior understanding of brand strategy and positioning

Competencies Required
- Superior collaborative relationship building
- Superior interpersonal skills, especially with the sales force
- Superior influencing abilities
- Solid creative and conceptual thinking
- Superior self-starter requiring limited supervision

Pros	Cons
👍 You have an important role in the organization that matters.	👎 This is a very specialized role involving only a portion of the 4 Ps of marketing.
👍 This is right brain/left brain role requiring strategic and creative thinking.	👎 Lots of internal selling is required to align all company stakeholders around a companywide brand strategy.
👍 You work with smart and highly motivated people.	👎 The job can require long hours and frequent travel.
👍 The results of your work can be seen by millions.	👎 There are a lot of "cooks in the kitchen," all with different opinions about the brand strategy. Your work is always being critiqued and challenged.
👍 This is a potential career path to chief marketing officer.	
👍 Your work involves fascinating areas, including market trends, cultural shifts, and consumer psychology.	👎 Usually not a career path to the C-suite.
👍 Good employment prospects. This is a highly specialized role gaining in prominence.	
👍 The pay can be very good.	

Career Path for the Corporate Brand Director

Corporate brand managers usually come up through the ranks of marketing—brand or product manager, marketing director. Corporate brand directors are also recruited from outside the company, often from an advertising agency and brand consultancy. Industry-specific knowledge, while helpful, is not necessarily a key criterion in hiring decisions. Most important is the ability to deeply assess customer perceptions of the brand and identify unique and differentiating insights that make the brand stand out from competitive offerings.

Your next career move in the organization could be into one of the company's product divisions as a director or VP of marketing. You will be in the running for the chief marketing officer position, especially if you gain product-marketing experience in one of the divisions.

Salaries

Corporate brand directors can expect to earn between $150k and $180k plus a 25% to 30% bonus (at companies with $1B+ revenue).

A Day in the Life of the Corporate Brand Director

8:00: Prepare for brand strategy presentation at national sales meeting

9:30: Leave office to drive to consumer research

10:00: Attend consumer focus group research regarding competitive brands

12:00: Lunch with market research team to discuss focus group findings

13:00: Present brand positioning and design standards to new marketing hires

> 15:00: Provide update to digital marketing team on new brand strategy
>
> 16:00: Meet with ad agency to review new TV advertising ideas
>
> 17:00: Prepare for evening call with Asia-Pacific regional brand team
>
> 17:30: Leave office to drive home
>
> 20:00: Present Asia-Pacific brand measurement results to regional team
>
> 21:00: Wrap up calls; agree action items to improve brand awareness in China

Landing Your First Job

Corporate brand management is not an entry-level position. It's essential that you first cut your teeth in a brand, product, or advertising management role to learn the fundamentals of brand strategy and brand positioning. You'll need at least 10 years of related experience before you would be considered to lead corporate brand management at a major company.

In the Final Analysis

Brand strategy can be a challenging concept for some businesspeople to grasp. So beware; this role is not always understood or appreciated. But the impact a great brand director can have on the value of the company is profound. Great companies and progressive CEOs understand and greatly value this. If you thrive on getting inside the customer's head and pure brand strategy, corporate brand management provides an excellent career opportunity.

See Appendix 1 for a list of great companies to begin your career with.

E-COMMERCE MARKETING

Global e-commerce sales are currently about $1.5 trillion and rising at a double-digit rate. Almost all growth occurring within retail is due to Internet versus physical store sales. What does that mean for you? It means that e-commerce is an incredible career opportunity with big upside growth potential.

E-commerce has completely changed the course of many industries. Media was the first impacted, as the convenience and value of buying online triggered the shuttering of most book, music, and video retailers. Showrooming—or the practice of checking out a product in the physical store and then buying it for the lowest possible price online—has resulted in big challenges for retailers in all industries, especially electronics.

But now even industries that seemed relatively sheltered from the e-commerce onslaught, such as the furniture and clothing, are getting very (very) nervous. There is no reversing the course. The only question is when e-commerce will simply be referred to as commerce.

There are many different career options within e-commerce, but this book focuses on roles that align squarely with the marketing profession: e-commerce manager (discussed in the Marketing Management section) and e-commerce merchandising manager (discussed in the Marketing Execution section).

E-Commerce Marketing Manager

The e-commerce marketing manager leads strategic planning and execution for a brand's or a retailer's online store. This is an extremely competitive space, and the e-commerce manager plays a critical role in the success or failure of the business.

The e-commerce marketing manager develops the e-commerce strategy determining what should be sold, how it is merchandised, and how it is priced. He then develops a promotional plan to find prospective buyers through digital advertising, search, and social media to motivate them to visit the company's website. The e-commerce manager then applies an assortment of tactics—pricing, promotions, product assortment—to motivate shoppers to select a product and place it in the e-shopping cart. Finally, it's the e-commerce manager's job to seal the deal and ensure the shoppers complete the purchase.

The great thing about e-commerce is that everything is measurable—every dollar spent can be evaluated against sales generated. The e-commerce manager relentlessly uses data to update and optimize company programs—literally on a daily or even hourly basis. It's an intense role with a clear end game.

E-commerce management responsibilities vary significantly by type of industry. A media company, such as Disney, defines the role differently than, say, a cosmetics company. Also, a pure-play e-retailer, such as Amazon, has somewhat different requirements than a retailer that sells both online and in physical stores, such as Walmart. However, core tenets of the job—strategy, execution, measurement, and optimization—always hold true and form the basis of our discussion.

Typical Job Description:
E-Commerce Marketing Manager

Formal Job Description	What This _REALLY_ Means
Lead strategic planning for the e-commerce program to achieve defined revenue and profitability goals.	You are on the hook to figure out how to continually grow the business in an ultracompetitive marketplace. It's your business to run.
Create the online merchandising plan determining the optimal product assortment, placement, pricing, and promotional activity.	You have many variables to consider when planning your program. You are on a continuous quest to find the perfect mix that maximizes sales and profitability.
Develop customer acquisition, conversion, and retention campaigns. Lead the execution of SEM, SEO, digital display advertising, web landing pages, social media, affiliate marketing, and e-mail marketing.	You need to have a strong grasp of the many subspecialties of digital marketing. You'll also need to have knowledge of the practice of inbound marketing.
Create online marketing campaigns for key seasonal and promotional events.	The majority of your sales will happen during a few key shopping seasons. This is make-or-break time for your business.
Analyze sales performance and continually optimize program performance utilizing A/B and multivariate testing.	Your customers leave clues every hour of every day about their needs and what they will buy. You must be a relentless tester and optimizer.
Be a thought leader in digital	Online shopping decision making

| trends, particularly those related to the online shopping experience. | remains a mystery. You are expected to be your company's foremost expert in this area. |

What You Need to Be Successful

Superior = mastery / Strong = much better than average / Solid = competitive

The successful e-commerce manager is a digital marketing expert as well as a retailer, entrepreneur, and shopper psychologist.

It goes without saying that an e-commerce manager must be fluent in all things digital. In addition to the basics (search marketing, web communication, digital advertising), the manager must also quickly embrace all new technologies, including social media, mobile marketing, and big data.

But the e-commerce manager is primarily a retailer operating in a digital marketplace. Deep knowledge of current and future industry trends is essential to inform the most appropriate product assortment. A wealth of experience in knowing what shoppers do and do not respond to in terms of pricing, promotions, and web content is critical. Also important is solid business judgment to create a marketing plan that invests company money in the most effective and efficient channels.

Lastly, a relentless thirst for shopper insights and marketing performance optimization separates the adequate from the superior e-commerce manager.

Skills Required
- Superior knowledge of digital marketing channels and technology
- Strong strategic thinking
- Strong quantitative thinking
- Strong project management
- Solid written and verbal communication

Competencies Required
- Strong collaborative relationship-building capabilities
- Strong ability to multitask and manage multiple priorities
- Strong team player
- Solid influencing skills

Pros	Cons
👍 This is the uber digital marketing role.	👎 Very competitive thus very stressful field.
👍 The job is both strategic and creative.	👎 Your work is never done.
👍 Your impact is highly measurable.	👎 Can be very long hours.
👍 Strong future employment potential.	👎 Employment security can sometimes be unpredictable.
👍 The pay can be very good.	
👍 Strong career potential.	
👍 Limited travel.	

Career Path for the e-Commerce Marketing Manager

E-commerce *is* the future of retailing and provides terrific long-term career opportunities. Depending on the size of the company, your career path could lead from manager to director to VP of e-commerce and, ultimately, to president of the company. But keep in mind that the competition in retailing, and especially online retailing, is brutal.

If the relentless pace of e-retailing becomes too much, you can easily make the transition to such roles as digital marketing manager. Of course, you will also be well prepared to run your own e-commerce business.

Salaries

Salaries for E-commerce marketing managers vary widely based on the size of the company and range between $50k and $100k plus a 10% to 30% bonus.

A Day in the Life of the E-Commerce Manager

8:00: Review overnight sales data

9:00: Meet with merchandising team to update product assortment

10:00: Prepare for quarterly sales results meeting to senior management

11:30: Meet with Google sales team to review SEM program results

13:00: Lunch at desk; catch up on e-mail

> 14:00: Meet with ad agency to review new digital advertising campaign
>
> 15:00: Meet with IT department to demo new shopping cart functionality
>
> 16:00: Plan multivariate test program for new product line with analytics team
>
> 17:00: Scan competitive websites for new merchandising programs

Landing Your First Job

E-Commerce is all about retailing in the digital space. Thus any retailing job (in a store or online) is a good first step. Your ability to demonstrate that you can think like a shopper and understand the shopper's needs and what triggers a sale will impress any potential employer.

One recommendation for getting your foot in the door is to write to a retail executive and provide your analysis of his company's online shopping experience and how you think it can be improved. What was your shopping goal before you landed on its website? What were your first impressions when you landed there? Were the items presented in an enticing way? What did the site do to convert you to an immediate sale? How was the checkout process compared to other e-retailers checkout? Online shopping behavior is a riddle inside a mystery, and no e-retailer understands this perfectly. Your ability to demonstrate an aptitude for such thinking should be held in high regard by a prospective employer.

Take note of the difference between pure-play e-commerce companies, such as amazon.com, that sell only online and do not have physical stores, and hybrid retailers like Walmart that sell both online and offline. Consider if your career ambitions are strictly online or if work in both online and offline retailing interests you.

In the Final Analysis

E-commerce is at the intersection of digital marketing and retailing and provides a dynamic, competitive, and exhilarating career choice. Not to mention the best possible training to run your own online business someday.

See Appendix 1 for a list of great companies to begin your career with.

Related Careers in E-Commerce

E-Commerce Merchandising Manager

Split-second purchase decisions are made by consumers when shopping online, and it is the responsibility of the e-commerce merchandising manager to adjust the product assortment, pricing, promotions, and other variables mix to maximize sales.

While the e-commerce manager is responsible for sales and profitability of the overall online store, the e-commerce merchandising manager optimizes sales conversion of specific pages of the site (usually a product category), ensuring that the right assortment of products is displayed and that the products are merchandised with the right photos, videos, and copy.

The e-commerce merchandising manager usually plans weekly and seasonal promotional offers and creates the content on the web pages to support them. The role requires extensive collaboration with the e-commerce, advertising, and search marketing teams to coordinate all merchandising activity. Continuous data measurement, analysis, and optimization are required to remain ahead of the curve in the ultracompetitive business of e-commerce.

A good e-commerce merchandising manager needs both a strategic and a creative mind. Strong analytical skills are a must, but a good eye for design is also necessary. The e-commerce merchandising manager needs to collaborate with various partners across the company, so teaming skills are essential. This role also requires strong project management skills and incredible attention to detail.

Direct Response Marketing Manager

With direct response marketing there is no middleman—no retailer, wholesaler, or other third party. The brand or company sells directly to the end customer through catalogs, direct mail, mass media and telemarketing.

This field has been completely redefined by digital marketing with e-mail, website, search marketing, social media, and mobile now added to (or replacing) the traditional mix of tactics. What remains constant is the use of data, testing, and relentless campaign optimization to drive customer calls to action to acquire new ones and to retain existing ones.

The direct response marketing manager leads planning, execution, measurement, and optimization of direct response marketing programs. She determines the product to be marketed and plans campaigns to acquire new customers (customer acquisition programs) or to get existing customers to buy again (customer relationship marketing programs). A key starting point for the manager is to segment the market based on customer data. Taking into consideration demographic (for example, age, income, education level), psychographic (for example, lifestyle interests, political affiliations) and past purchasing data, the direct response marketer organizes potential customers into various segments (groups). The manager then creates a marketing program that customizes product assortment, pricing, advertising, and promotion for each segment.

Often the direct marketing manager works with an advertising agency to plan the promotional material and to select media. A key part of the job is to design A/B and multivariate testing that tests alternative tactics to get customers to act.

- Which offer best drives response, the free gift bag or buy two get one free offer?
- Which copy in the ad results in the most calls, limited time offer or money back guarantee?
- Which e-mail headline generates the most clicks, 33% off or free shipping?

With the answers to these and up to a dozen other tests running simultaneously, the manager is continually analyzing campaign performance and optimizing the marketing mix.

Effective direct response marketers are serial optimizers and crave finding ways to increase customer response. This role requires strong strategic thinking capabilities and advanced analytical and data-mining skills. You will also need top organizational skills to thrive in a complex and fast-moving work environment.

MARKETING EXECUTION

In contrast to marketing management, marketing execution roles focus on expert planning and implementation of a single component of the marketing mix. Whether advertising, consumer promotion, or marketing at the point of sale, these specialized positions are where "the rubber meets the road' since the best marketing strategy is worthless without executional excellence.

The Marketing Funnel

A great framework to evaluate marketing execution career opportunities is the marketing funnel. The funnel metaphor is used to describe how marketers guide consumers through various stages of marketing activity that leads to an initial sales and ongoing brand loyalty.

There are four sections within the funnel, each representing a primary objective of any marketing communication plan: Awareness. Consideration, Acquisition and Loyalty

The Marketing Funnel

The top of the funnel focuses on finding potential buyers and creating a positive impression about the brand. Of course, you can't create a positive impression until the customer knows your brand exists. So the first objective of any communication program (and thus the marketing funnel) is to create brand awareness (funnel Stage 1). Once this is established, the marketer then explains what the brand offers and why the customer should consider buying it. Consideration is the second stage of the marketing funnel and is where the marketer communicates the brand's distinctive product benefits and features. Marketing roles at the top of the funnel include advertising, media, and web communications.

The middle of the funnel (Stage 3) is called either the *trial* or *acquisition* stage. Assuming your prospective customer is aware and considering your product, the objective here is to prompt some type of customer action that will directly or indirectly lead to a sale. Marketing communication professionals who work at this stage implement a variety of programs to motivate prospects to sample a product, use a coupon, call the sales center, or request more product information. Expertise in this area (lead generation) is the hottest area of marketing now and has been revolutionized by digital media and technologies.

The bottom of the funnel (fourth stage) is referred to as loyalty, and focuses on reactivating sales among the brands existing customer base. As we'll discuss, it is much more profitable for a brand to maintain a loyal customer than it is to find a new one—much more profitable. This book reviews customer relationship management, another hot career track with excellent potential.

ADVERTISING MANAGEMENT

With the typical consumer exposed to more than 5,000 advertising and brand messages per day, and with the insane proliferation of digital and social channels, competition for mind share has never been greater. The art and science of advertising is about creating memorable and compelling messages that stand out in this cluttered media landscape.

This book provides the client-side view of advertising, the management of an in-house staff of advertising specialists or outside ad agencies. As noted, this profession typically focuses on the top of the marketing funnel to create brand awareness and consideration via TV, print, radio, outdoor, and digital media. Here, we focus on two core positions: advertising manager (director) and media manager (director).

Advertising Manager

The advertising manager is responsible for leading the planning, creation, execution, and measurement of the brand's integrated advertising program. *Integrated* means the holistic planning of any and all types of advertising—TV, print, digital, outdoor, radio. All these channels must work together to have the greatest influence on consumer perceptions.

Advertising managers need to do many things really well, including lead a team of specialists to create and distribute great advertising. She first writes the advertising brief that directs the activities of the advertising creative, production, and media teams. A lot is riding on the accuracy and clarity of this brief that must address a host of questions such as:

- Who is the advertising intended for?
- What key message is it to deliver?
- What claims should be made, and why should the consumer believe them?
- What's the budget?
- When should the advertising run?

With this information, the ad agency or in-house ad team is directed by the ad manager to develop creative ideas which she then assesses against a number of criteria including:
- Is the creative idea on strategy?
- Is there a big idea that will make the ad stand out?
- Will it connect with the target audience?
- Will the campaign have legs and be able to work far into the future?

The advertising manager also reviews the media plan, taking a variety of factors into consideration.
- How is the budget allocated across different types of media (the media mix) such as network TV, cable TV, print, and digital.
- Is the advertising reaching the intended target audience an appropriate number times?
- What is the quality and reputation of the specific media properties (TV shows, magazine titles, websites etc.) and are they a good fit with the brand's image
- How cost effective is the media plan? Is the brand getting the most ad exposures for the available budget?

The advertising manager also needs to measure the impact of the advertising by executing copy research in partnership with the market researcher. Finally, she needs to sell the advertising program to a variety of people within the company, chief among them the chief marketing officer. This is not always an easy task since often "beauty is in the eye of the beholder."

Typical Job Description: Advertising Manager

Formal Job Description	What This _REALLY_ Means
Lead the planning of integrated advertising campaigns in support of overall marketing objectives.	You are a key player on the marketing team with huge responsibility for the success of the brand or company.
Manage the in-house team or external advertising agency to plan, create, and execute advertising campaigns, ensuring all work is on strategy.	You will (usually) work with an amazing team of really smart people from really different backgrounds with really strong opinions. It's your job to get everyone pointed in the right direction and to get the best out of them.
Write clear advertising briefs to guide all advertising development.	You don't just go make an ad. It's critical that everyone knows the goal of the ad, the target audience, and the key messages (brand benefits) the advertising should be deliver.
Strive to deliver the big advertising idea enabling the brand to stand out in a cluttered media landscape.	Most ads are good but not great. You need to do everything in your power to get the ad agency to deliver that "1 in a 100" campaign.

Direct the media team to develop innovative programs that reach consumers with the right message at the right time at the right place.	The big money in advertising is spent on media. You need to be certain that this money is spent in the most effective and efficient way.
Gain internal approvals of advertising concepts to senior management, legal, and other company stakeholders.	You have a lot of work to do to gain buy-in for your ad campaign. This takes a lot of perseverance because everyone thinks they are an ad expert.
Manage production of audio-visual (video/film/photo) shoots relating to brand and advertising campaigns.	You will have specialists working for you who write, produce, and edit the advertising. But you need to get them to work in unison.
Lead the planning of advertising and media measurement research.	One way or another you need to prove that your advertising is having a positive impact. Otherwise, you won't get funded.
Manage budgets for ad production, media, and research.	These can be huge budgets, so serious attention to detail is necessary.

What You Need to Be Successful

Superior = mastery / Strong = much better than average / Solid = competitive

A superior advertising manager is truly a left brain/right brain person. She needs to be able to judge creativity but also dig deep into analytics. She needs to relate to and motivate a cast of characters ranging from creative directors to copywriters to media planners to video producers. Being a strong salesperson to gain buy-in for ad programs is also helpful. The campaign idea goes nowhere unless executive management gives the green light.

Finally, a superior advertising manager has an insatiable thirst to find the big idea and that special connection to the customer. Discovering unique insights into the customer's unspoken needs and motivations is the "secret sauce" of exceptional advertising.

Skills Required
- Superior creative and conceptual thinking
- Strong strategic thinking capabilities
- Strong understanding of marketing strategy and brand positioning
- Strong project management
- Superior written and verbal communication

Competencies Required
- Superior influencing skills
- Superior ability to building collaborative relationships
- Strong ability to motivate others

Pros	Cons
👍 A highly visible and important role in most companies.	👎 The job is frequently very stressful.
👍 The most purely creative role of all marketing career options.	👎 Everyone has an opinion about your work.
👍 Millions of people see the results of your work every	👎 There can be long hours during key times.
	👎 Employment security can sometimes be unpredictable.

day.	☞ This is not a path to executive management on the client side.
👍 You work with a vast array of talented people.	
👍 The pay can be very good.	☞ Work/life balance can frequently be challenging.

Career Path for the Advertising Manager

Typically, a client-side advertising manager has some ad agency work experience. The role is also a specialized area of marketing, so the career path is relatively limited. An advertising manager (responsible for a single brand or area of the business) can move to advertising director or VP of advertising leading advertising for a portfolio of brands or the entire company. He can also move into marketing management (brand or product management) since advertising skills provide an ideal foundation for these positions.

Salaries

Salaries vary significantly, depending on the size of the company. But advertising managers at large companies can expect to earn between $80k and $120k plus a 20% to 25% bonus.

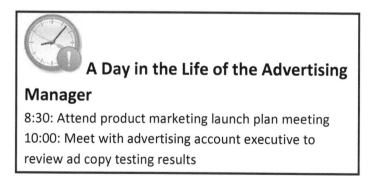

A Day in the Life of the Advertising Manager

8:30: Attend product marketing launch plan meeting
10:00: Meet with advertising account executive to review ad copy testing results

11:00: Review talent reel to find new brand TV spokesperson

12:00: Lunch with magazine sales rep

13:00: Receive debrief from media team on key media measurements

14:00: Lead team workshop to assess new cultural trends

15:00: Review ad production estimate for TV ad shoot

16:00: Meet with Facebook ad reps to review new ad models

17:00: Prep for tomorrow's new campaign update to the marketing VP

Landing Your First Job

If advertising management appeals to you as a career option, you should pursue both
client-side and agency-side opportunities. There is no cookie-cutter approach to activating an advertising career, and the industry is notoriously difficult to land one's first job. The glamour of advertising attracts many of the best and brightest competing for a handful of low-paying entry-level jobs. So look for any type of position, whether in media, research, or even an administrative role. This is frequently the first step in the advertising management career journey.

Effective networking is the key to landing your first job. You will need to aggressively find fellow alumni, friends, neighbors, or others to help secure an informational interview at an ad agency or company. Target your efforts by reading *Ad Age* and other industry press to learn those brands investing in new advertising

Once you have secured an interview, it's very important to
articulate your motivations for pursuing this career and how
your experiences and skills position you for success. You must
become a student of great advertising and marketing.
Constantly critique the ads you see on TV, in magazines, or on
online: What was the big idea in the advertising? Was there
even a big idea? Who is the intended target audience? What
was the key message and was the ad memorable? Having a
well-considered point of view should give you a leg up in
landing your first job.

In the Final Analysis

Advertising management is a great career option for those
looking to work in the most creative part of business. There's a
lot of pressure, but there's good pay and never a dull moment.

See Appendix 1 for a list of great companies to begin your career
with.

Related Careers in Advertising

Media Management

The majority of media career positions reside in ad agencies or media buying agencies. Client-side media career opportunities generally exist in companies with very large advertising budgets. These roles are responsible for understanding the media placement needs of all the brands within the company (their objectives, goals, budgets, timing) and for directing the planning and implementation of media planning and buying.

Media management includes evaluating the media mix and the allocation of the budget across various types of media. The role directs the media plan's reach and frequency to ensure that the target audience is sufficiently exposed to the ads. The manager also assesses the quality and reputation of the media properties being considered and evaluates the cost efficiency of the media plan to get the most ad exposure for the available budget.

Media management has changed radically with the emergence of the digital era. In the old days, a typical media program consisted of television advertising, some print advertising, and perhaps a smattering of radio and outdoor advertising. There are now an overwhelming number of media channels, including mobile and social, and formats, including online video, for the advertiser to consider. Digital has also ushered in a new era of advertising that includes not only display (banner) advertising but also highly sophisticated approaches, such as behavioral advertising, remarketing, and contextual advertising.

Media management requires excellent quantitative skills combined with an intuitive understanding of how people engage with various types of media. The field has changed dramatically over the last decade and will continue to do so driven by the impact of digital. If you have an intuitive grasp of digital and social media and strong analytical skills you are poised well for future success in media management.

Consumer Promotion Management

Consumer promotion management plans and implements a wide spectrum of activities all geared to driving consumer trial and repeat purchase. This includes executing old-school tactics, such as couponing via the Sunday paper, direct mail, or on-product packaging; contests; and in-store sampling programs. Digital media and technology have also spurred a new generation of highly engaging (and viral) promotional activities.

Consumer promotion is a core function within consumer goods companies and is essential for maintaining the existing customer base and for continually bringing new customers into the franchise.

Consumer Promotion Manager

The consumer promotion manager is assigned to a brand or group of brands and leads the planning and implementation of all consumer promotion programs. The manager usually report to a consumer promotion director but takes overall business direction from the brand manager.

The consumer promotion manager leads promotion planning and identifies creative ways to obtain trial among new users, inducing them with various offers to try the product: couponing, sampling, games & contests, special offers etc. He must also ensure that current customers keep buying the product. Customer lifetime value is a marketing approach grounded on the simple principle that a minority of a brand's customers, the most valuable customers (MVCs), are responsible for the overwhelming majority of the brand's profits. The consumer promotion manager works relentlessly to build this pool of MVCs while ensuring that current MVCs stay loyal to the brand.

Most of the field implementation work (sampling programs, in-store events etc.) is done by outside vendors but it is the consumer promotion manager's job to hire them and coordinate their activities.

Typical Job Description:
Consumer Promotion Manager

Formal Job Description	What This _REALLY_ Means
Lead the planning and execution of promotional programs to stimulate trial and ongoing consumer purchases.	Your ability to gain sufficient trial and ongoing repeat sales is crucial to the success of the business. And your competition is brutal!
Create consumer promotion programs that support defined marketing objectives and are aligned to advertising, trade promotion, and other marketing communication.	You're playing on a team, and you need to be completely coordinated with all the other team members to run the play. Expect lots of meetings to iron this out.
Conceptualize highly creative promotions that help differentiate the brand in the marketplace.	The world is really cluttered with brand promotions, and you are expected to keep coming up with ideas that are truly unique.

Plan, execute, and measure promotional programs (discounts, samples, gifts, rebates, coupons, sweepstakes, contests) via direct mail, inserts in newspapers, digital media, in-store displays, product endorsements, or special events.	You have a wide variety of options at your disposal to get the consumer to buy the product. You need to find the right mix of tactics that does it cost efficiently.
Present promotional plans to marketing, sales, and senior management.	You will always need to pitch your wares. But note that the bar for innovative and effective ideas keeps getting raised.
Recruit and manage external vendors supporting promotional programs.	Most of the tedious work of promotions will be done by outside parties, but you will need to choose really good partners and manage them closely.
Leverage social media as a promotional channel and be the thought leader for innovative and creative approaches to consumer promotion.	Marketers have yet to realize the potential of social media and technology as a promotional weapon. You have the opportunity to invent the future of this profession.

What You Need to Be Successful

Superior = mastery / Strong = much better than average / Solid = competitive

Superior promotion managers are smart, creative, and highly energetic. They are passionate about finding new ways to connect with and influence consumers. They are also highly detail oriented because their programs often reach tens of millions of customers and there is no margin for error.

> Consider the true story of one win-a-new-car promotion. The program offered a new car to the holder of the one special key that started the car. Unfortunately, some poor promotion manager allowed thousands of keys to be distributed to consumers—each of them started the car!

Skills Required

- Superior project management
- Strong customer orientation
- Solid understanding of marketing strategy and brand positioning
- Solid written and verbal communication skills
- Solid strategic thinking capabilities

Competencies Required

- Strong conceptual and creative thinking
- Strong teamwork capabilities
- Strong ability to build collaborative relationships
- Solid influencing skills

Pros	Cons
It's both a strategic and creative role.	Often highly stressful.
Your work influences the actions of millions of people.	Pay is good but not as good as other in marketing areas.
There is always opportunity	Can be long hours during

to create something new.	key times.
👍 This role is somewhat less competitive than other marketing roles.	👎 Not a path to executive management.
👍 Solid employment prospects.	

Career Path for the Consumer Promotion Manager

Consumer promotion management is a highly specialized career and is not a path to senior management. You will typically start as a promotion assistant working for a promotion manager. You will move up to the manager level after two or three years. After five or more years as a manager, the next (and usually final) rung on the ladder is consumer promotion director. Of course, it's entirely possible to make a lateral move into brand or product marketing if you're interested in options that offer a path to executive management.

Salaries

Consumer promotion managers can expect to earn $75k to $120k plus a 15% to 20% bonus at companies with $1 billion or more in annual sales revenue.

A Day in the Life of the Consumer Promotion Manager

8:30: Attend product marketing launch plan meeting
10:00: Meet with promotion vendor to discuss in-store sampling program

---

11:00: Present holiday program couponing plan to brand manager

12:00: Lunch with sales director

13:00: Review brand loyalty research results; brainstorm new loyalty programs

15:00: Lead team workshop to assess new promotion trends

16:00: Meet with social media manager to review Facebook promotional programs

17:00: Prep for tomorrow's holiday promotion presentation to senior   management

Landing Your First Job

Promotion management is a very good entry-level job that does not require an MBA or master's degree. But it can be a highly competitive to land a role with a marquee company. Key to landing the first role is strongly articulating what attracts you to this field:

- Why intrigues you about consumer promotion?
- What do you know about this kind of work?
- Why would you be a good fit?
- What are your favorite promotions, and which have influenced you to buy the brand?

You probably have had some promotional experience in your lifetime—any job that involved getting someone to try something new. Find an experience or two from your past that might serve as a reference point for promotional experience. And remember the ever-important need to shine in self-promotion. Besides your résumé, think of other creative ways to promote yourself to the hiring manager.

> A great friend from Unilever landed his job
> there by shipping his résumé to the promotion
> director responsible for Promise margarine in
> an empty tub of the product. Inside a note read,
> "I Promise to be the best promotion assistant
> you ever hired." He was immediately called in
> for an interview and hired on the spot!

In the Final Analysis

Consumer promotion management provides another excellent option for the creatively minded and detail oriented. The pay is good, but career advancement maxes out at mid management.

See Appendix 1 for a list of great companies to begin your career with.

TRADE MARKETING

Trade marketing is an essential function for companies that sell indirectly. That means their products are first sold to a third party who in turn sells to the final customer. A B2C company must first sell to a Walmart or CVS, whereas B2B companies must first sell to various business partners who serve as middlemen distributors.

Trade promotion marketers develop programs to secure distribution for the product at the retailer or channel partner. Once the product is in distribution, trade promotion marketing is about supporting that retailer or channel partner to successfully sell it to the end customer. Thus programs are developed that define pricing, promotions, and other incentives that drive revenue for both the trade partner and the company.

B2C marketing is divided into push and pull promotional activities. Pull means those marketing activities seen by consumers outside of the retail environment to motivate them to "pull" the product off the store shelf—mainly advertising and consumer promotion programs. Push marketing is another term for trade marketing and refers to programs designed to get retailers to "push" the product to consumers at the point of sale—mainly through promotion incentives, pricing discounts, and special display programs.

B2B companies often refer to trade marketing activities as channel marketing. Tech companies, such as IBM, sell hardware and software to an array of channel partners, including software developers, IT system integrators, and other resellers. This requires dedicated marketing programs to induce these channel partners to include the product as part of their offerings to the end customer. Marketing programs are customized to offer the right set of products, pricing, and promotion incentives to the channel partners.

Trade Promotion Marketing Manager

As noted, this role is all about pushing products at retail and requires having one foot in sales and another foot in marketing. Why is this trade promotion such an important role? Despite all the effort and expense to build a loyal customer base, the overwhelming majority of the time the consumer simply does not perceive significant differentiation between the top brands within any given category. Every hour of every day the store shelf is *the* decisive battleground for winning sales and market share.

B2C trade promotion focuses on the planning and implementation of price promotions (i.e. what's on sale this week), special in-store placements (such as end-aisle displays), and special promotions (for example, buy one get one free). The trade promotion manager works on a national or regional basis and manages promotions for a specific product category, such as hair care, across multiple types of retailers, such as supermarkets, drug stores, and big box retailers. The manager directs the flow of millions of dollars of the company's money to develop programs for retail partners that maximize sales velocity while delivering acceptable profit margins. Promote the product too aggressively with a deep discounted price, and the company loses money on each unit sold (not a good business practice, to say the least). Promote the product too conservatively, and sales goals are not met (also not a good thing).

The trade promotion manager sits in the real-world hot seat—with consumers voting each day about her performance with their purchases.

Typical Job Description:
Trade Promotion Marketing Manager (B2C)

Formal Job Description	What This _REALLY_ Means
Partner with sales and marketing to develop customer-specific strategies that integrate sales plans, product plans, and marketing objectives.	You need to work with both the obnoxious marketing people and the impatient salespeople. Both depend on you to deliver the right programs to drive sales.
Develop retail account-specific short-term and long-term trade promotion business plans.	You need to have a good business mind and balance many factors, including often incompatible sales quota and profit expectations.
Build strong, trusting partner-based relationships with key retail account managers, the sales force, and the marketing teams.	For any business relationship to work, all parties involved must feel that they are benefiting. It's your job to find the right equation that delivers for both your company and the retailer.
Lead the planning for retail product assortment, merchandising, and trade promotions.	No two retailers are the same. Each needs a marketing program customized to meet the needs of

	the consumer, the retailer, and the brand.
Develop the promotion and merchandising calendar for retail accounts and ensure alignment with consumer promotion, advertising, and other marketing activities.	When push marketing programs work synergistically with the brand's advertising and consumer promotion, pull marketing programs results increase dramatically.
Lead trade promotion measurement and analysis, and report results versus objectives to senior sales and marketing management.	Just because you are no longer in school does not mean that you don't get a report card! You will have access to reams of data to assess the success or failure of your work.

What You Need to Be Successful

Superior = mastery / Strong = much better than average / Solid = competitive

The best trade promotion managers are superior salespeople with sharp strategic instincts. Relationships matter greatly, and the managers must build and maintain a strong rapport with retailer partners as well as the sales force. This means truly understanding their respective goals and being an advocate to achieve win-win outcomes. Sometimes these needs come in conflict with the expectations of the brand, and it's the trade promotion manager's role to sort it out.

Skills Required
- Strong understanding of the retail trade promotion planning process
- Superior analytical thinking
- Strong project management

91

- Solid strategic thinking
- Solid written and verbal communication
- Solid understanding of consumer marketing activities

Competencies Required
- Superior ability to build collaborative relationships
- Superior influencing skills
- Strong teamwork capabilities

Pros	Cons
👍 It's an important job with significant responsibility and budget.	👎 It's a very specialized and focused role.
👍 Excellent experience for a career in brand management or sales.	👎 Balancing the needs of the retailer, the sales force, and the business can be challenging.
👍 The job is one part corporate and one part sales.	👎 There is constant tension between driving sales and profit.
👍 The impact of your work is measurable.	👎 The pay is good but usually not as good as a field sales position's pay.
👍 This can be a path to senior sales and marketing management.	👎 The constant analysis and reporting can be a grind.
👍 There is usually good work/life balance.	

Career Path for the Trade Promotion Marketing Manager

From my experience, trade promotion management is not a dedicated career path but serves as a valuable, but temporary, career development stint. Usually, high potential sales reps are offered these roles as stepping stones to future senior levels of management. The role will test their strategic and analytical skills and their ability to work and communicate effectively within a corporate environment.

Salaries

Trade marketing managers can expect to earn $80k to $130k plus a 25% to 30% bonus at companies with $1 billion dollars or more in annual sales revenue.

A Day in the Life of the Trade Promotion Manager

8:30: Attend product marketing launch plan meeting

10:00: Meet with brand manager to plan Walmart product assortment strategy

11:00: Meet with consumer promotion to review holiday promo couponing plan

12:00: Lunch with local market sales rep

13:00: Debrief from market research on shopper marketing study results

15:00: Analyze results of last month's Walmart in-store program

---

> 16:00: Finalize the special holiday trade promotion program
>
> 17:00: Answer calls and e-mail from field sales reps
>
> 18:00: Meet sales buddies in town for dinner

Landing Your First Job

Trade promotion roles are not usually entry-level positions, although assistant merchandising and trade analyst roles are sometimes available. Virtually all trade promotion managers have solid experience as field sales reps or were recruited from the marketing ranks. My advice is to first pursue an entry-level sales or sales analyst jobs and then seek a two-year assignment in trade marketing at a later point in your career.

In the Final Analysis

Trade promotion management is a great temporary gig to learn the big picture view of the industry, to see how things operate at headquarters, and to work side by side with the marketing team. This provides invaluable experience for future advancement within the sales or marketing organization.

See Appendix 1 for a list of great companies to begin your career with.

SHOPPER MARKETING

Shopper marketing was developed by fast-moving consumer goods companies, such as Procter & Gamble, acknowledging the obvious fact that local tastes impact buying preferences and behaviors.

- Do shoppers who live in wealthy neighborhoods respond to retail promotions the same way as shoppers in less affluent ones?
- Do shoppers in Boston suburbs behave the same as those in Atlanta?
- Is purchasing behavior in a college town different than in a retirement community?

Some things are similar, but many are not because of regional, cultural, economic, and other influences. Understanding and applying these insights to influence in-store sales is the role of the shopper marketer.

Shopper Marketing Manager

Shopper marketers must understand local shopping dynamics and then plan and implement retail marketing programs to increase brand sales.

- How do consumers plan their overall shopping?
- How do they navigate the supermarket or drug store aisles?
- What brands are in their consideration set as they shop a particular category?
- What in-store variables influence their selection of specific products?

- How sensitive are they to price discounts?

With these insights, the shopper marketer creates customized in-store programs to maximize brand sales. She might change the product assortment in the store based on local tastes, or partner with a complementary brand to create an end-aisle display, for example, pairing her company's potato chip brand with a dip brand that caters to regional tastes. Shopper marketing programs also include in-store sampling and special events, such as cooking classes or contests. The job offers many opportunities to creatively drive brand results.

> The Grocery Manufacturers Association published a study indicating that 70% of brand selections are made while at the store. So it's no surprise that fast-moving consumer goods companies are investing significantly in shopper marketing. Done right, shopper marketing can significantly impact sales. No wonder it's a growing field with a solid future.

The shopper marketer gains shopping insights by using store-level scanner data derived from each product's UPC (Universal Product Code) found on the package. These data provide highly detailed information about what is purchased in a specific store, at what price, and through which promotions. The shopper marketer uses these data to relentlessly improve the product assortment, pricing, and promotional programs to maximize brand sales.

Typical Job Description:
Shopper Marketing Manager

Formal Job Description	What This _REALLY_ Means
Lead planning, execution, and measurement for shopper marketing strategies and tactics that meet or exceed established business goals.	You will be accountable for meeting aggressive sales goals in a highly competitive environment. It's frightening and exhilarating!
Plan and execute the calendar of promotional tactics, including in-store media, trial-inducing promotional programs, product sampling, direct mail, and event marketing.	You have a blank canvas upon which to make your mark on the retail marketing of the brand. Ample opportunity to show your strategic and creative sides.
Develop a leading-edge understanding of the brand's consumers and their shopping needs and in-store purchasing behaviors.	You will be competing with very smart people who work for your competitor. Your ability to find deeper shopper insights will be key to your brand's sales success and your career success.
Strategically allocate the shopper marketing budget for optimal return on investment.	You will perpetually be on the quest for the perfect marketing mix. This mix changes constantly based on many factors, and you will need to adjust your tactics to maximize sales.
Hire and supervise third-party vendors in support of promotional	You will rely on others to manage the detailed executional

programs.	legwork of your plan. They will have other clients that are demanding their time—you need to get more than your fair share of their time!
Optimize the brand experience at the point of sale.	There is likely a multimillion dollar campaign supporting the brand. The brand's presentation at retail should reinforce and complement this investment and better not look cheesy.

What You Need to Be Successful

Superior = mastery / Strong = much better than average / Solid = competitive

The shopper marketer needs a solid combination of street-level and strategic thinking capabilities. An intuitive understanding of the deals, products, and in-store communication that trigger a purchase decision is the key ingredient to success. The shopper marketer also sits at the intersection of the brand, the sales force, and the customer. So the ability to mediate their respective objectives to create win-win-win outcomes is critical.

Skills Required
- Strong project management
- Strong understanding of the retail trade promotion-planning process
- Solid understanding of consumer marketing activities
- Solid creative problem solving

- Solid analytical thinking
- Solid knowledge of local ethnic and cultural trends

Competencies Required
- Superior customer orientation and passion for understanding shopping behavior
- Strong influencing skills
- Strong ability to build collaborative relationships
- Strong decision-making skills

Pros	Cons
👍 It's an important job with significant responsibility and budget.	👎 It's a very specialized role.
👍 Excellent experience for a career in brand management or sales.	👎 Balancing the needs of the retailer, the sales force, and the business can be challenging.
👍 The job is one part corporate and one part sales.	👎 There is constant tension between driving sales and profit.
👍 The impact of your work is measurable.	👎 This is not a career path to executive management.
👍 You are based in the field without day-to-day corporate oversight.	👎 The pay is decent but not as good as a sales or brand marketing position's pay.
👍 The job usually provides decent work/life balance.	

Career Path for the Shopper Marketing Manager

Shopper marketing will continue to grow in stature, but your career will max out at middle management. That said, it's a terrific role to gain an unmatched understanding of the consumer and retail—solid foundations to move laterally into brand marketing, sales, and even consumer insight (market research) career paths.

Salaries

Shopper marketers can expect to earn $75k to $125k plus a 20% to 25% bonus.

A Day in the Life of the Shopper Marketer Manager

8:30: Attend the launch plan meeting for a new product introduction

10:00: Meet with regional sales director to review last quarter's key account results

11:00: Conference call consumer promotion manager to discuss sampling plan

12:00: Lunch with the local sales rep

13:00: Receive debrief from market research on shopper marketing study results

15:00: Analyze the results of last month's Walmart end-aisle display program

16:00: Finalize the special holiday trade promotion program

17:00: Answer calls and e-mails from field sales reps

Landing Your First Job

Shopper marketing jobs are available within FMCG (fast-moving consumer goods) companies. A college degree in marketing or sales administration combined with any kind of sales, consumer promotion, or retail experience is a great foundation.

As you interview for entry-level positions you will need to demonstrate your ability to think from the shopper's point of view. What unplanned purchase did you make recently in a grocery or drug store? What factors (brand reputation, price, the display placement) made you stop and look and ultimately confirm your decision to buy? There is no right or wrong answer to these questions, but this is the kind of thinking that will impress any prospective employer.

In the Final Analysis

Understanding how things work at the street level is a valuable function and skill set. Shopper marketing can provide you with an in-demand career opportunity or position you well to climb the sales or marketing ladder.

Related Careers in Shopper Marketing

Merchandising Manager

(Also Called In-Store Experience Manager)
The term *merchandising manager* is frequently used to describe a similar role to the shopper marketer outside of FMCG. So you will see this term used in book, clothing, and

electronics retailers, among others. While the retail environments are vastly different, the same principles of driving profitable sales by understanding consumer in-store shopping dynamics are at the center of the position. Translating these into the right product assortment, pricing, and promotional programs is essential to the success of the retailer.

EVENT MARKETING

Event marketing is about the design and execution of live, in-person events and exhibits that promote a product or a company. An event can be as simple as a booth at a trade show or as dramatic as huge Hollywood-like production in a major arena. This is a dynamic career option that has one foot in show business and the other in marketing.

Business-to-business companies frequently stage large events to promote their services or introduce new products. For many companies, event marketing is a core component of their marketing mix. Information technology and health care are two industries that rely heavily on these major gatherings to present their wares in the best possible light to industry influencers and key purchase decision makers. The outcome of these events is often make-or-break activities with respect to the sales. Apple and Samsung, for example, invest millions in massive events to introduce their latest rounds of innovations. These events are attended by thousands of people, including the investment community and the international news media, and stock prices rise and fall as the new lineup is unveiled.

Events are real time with little margin for error in their planning and implementation. Also, the bar keeps getting raised in terms of the quality and "wow factor" expected by attendees. This career path can indeed be a high-pressure path but one filled with significant opportunities for creativity with ample ability to make a significant impact on the business.

Event Marketing Manager

Event managers are responsible for the planning, execution, and measurement of a variety of customer-facing live events. These include industry trade shows—such as the annual Consumer Electronics Show in Las Vegas—company- specific events, and traveling road shows that are exclusive to the company's products.

Activities include management of all or some of the aspects of an event, including finding the location (hotel, resort, or other venue), determining the agenda, booking speakers and entertainment, arranging for food and beverages, managing the press, coordinating registration, and managing a host of specialized third-party vendors for such things as stage lighting and audio-visual needs.

The goal of the event manager is to make every program a truly exciting and memorable one while ensuring that everything runs smoothly. The event manager must also consider how to measure the success of the event based on feedback from customer and company participants.

Typical Job Description:
Event Marketing Manager

Formal Job Description	What This _REALLY_ Means
Lead planning for all customer trade shows, exhibits, road shows, and important internal company events.	There are many events within a given year, and they require a significant amount of upfront planning. Even though events are

	real time, their planning is not.
Coordinate all event logistics activities, including venue management, food and beverages, speaker and staging coordination, and audio-visual requirements.	The complexities and logistics of events cannot be underestimated. Your job is to be the quarterback and pull it all together.
Ensure that event themes support the overall marketing objectives, strategy, and brand positioning. Ensure event signage and graphics are properly branded aligning to corporate brand identity.	Events deliver an overall experience and thus positive or negative brand perception to the attendees. This experience must be in harmony with the advertising, promotions, and other ways attendees are exposed to the brand or company.
Establish quantifiable objectives for the event.	You'll need data to prove that attendees enjoyed the event, believed it was well run, and that it was better than that of your competitors' events.
Manage the event budget and negotiations with third-party vendors.	You will need to be a tough negotiator every single time!
Recruit, train, and supervise event/booth staff and third-party vendors.	The heavy lifting will be done by contractors that you will hire on a temporary basis. They will need intense oversight by you to do the job well.

Be a thought leader in the latest trends and technologies in event marketing.	Every year expectations increase to do something new and trendy and to increase the "wow factor." You must stay on top of your game.

What You Need to Be Successful

Superior = mastery/ Strong = much better than average / Solid = competitive

Superior event marketers are tireless perfectionists and are never satisfied with just putting on a good event. They see every event as a new challenge to run an even smoother program and to deliver an even higher level of attendee satisfaction. They must understand the big picture and consider how overall business goals can be facilitated through the event.

- Is the business goal to introduce a new product, to reward current loyal customers, or to communicate news to the press?
- What should the tone and manner of the event be? Formal? Fun?
- How is the company's brand image best represented through the event presentation?

Above all, the event marketing manager must have superior organization and multitasking skills and be able to effectively manage the wide variety of third-party vendors required to support all aspects of the event.

Skills Required
- Superior project management
- Strong negotiation skills

- Solid understanding of marketing strategy
- Solid abilities as a creative problem solver
- Solid communication and interpersonal skills

Competencies Required
- Superior collaborative relationship building
- Strong ability to motivate others
- Strong ability to adapt to change
- Solid influencing skills

Pros	Cons
An exciting and dynamic job.	It's a very specialized role.
A critical marketing function within B2B companies.	The job can be highly stressful because of the unpredictability of live events.
The job is one part corporate and one part show business.	It's not a career path to executive management.
The results of your work are experienced by many.	Good pay but on the lower end of the marketing pay scale.
Frequent travel, often to nice locations.	Some travel will likely require weekends away from home.
Good job stability.	

Career Path for the Event Marketing Manager

Event marketing is a highly specialized career and does not provide a path to senior management. You will likely start as an assistant manager and support one specific event activity at any given time. You will work your way up to manager after two to three years and manage the planning and execution of multiple events throughout the year. Career progression is typically capped as a director leading event marketing activities across the entire company.

Despite the rise of digital technologies, face-to-face meetings will remain an essential component of the marketing mix for many marketers. Event marketing provides a solid career option that is dynamic and rewarding. There are also ample opportunities to move from the client side to event management agencies and vendors where the pay is often more lucrative.

Salaries

Event marketing managers can expect to earn $70k to $100k plus a 15% to 20% bonus at companies with $1 billion dollars or more in annual sales revenue.

A Day in the Life of the Event Marketing Manager

8:30: Receive update from marketing on the new product launch plans

10:00: Meet with sales director to finalize annual sales meeting invitation list

11:00: Review attendee satisfaction survey results from last week's local trade show

12:00: Lunch with corporate brand director to review new brand guidelines

> 13:00: Review capabilities of potential vendors for next year's Vegas trade show
> 15:00: Finalize report to the event director on last quarter's customer road show
> 16:00: Review webcasting platform options with info technology team
> 17: 00: Meet with audio-visual vendor to prepare for annual investor conference
> 19:00: Leave for airport to scout potential resorts for the annual sales meeting

Landing Your First Job

Employers will be looking for smart candidates with a high degree of passion for the profession and who have demonstrated exceptional organizational and interpersonal skills. They will also be looking for candidates with a high energy level and who work well under extreme pressure and tight timelines.

You can easily get event management experience by volunteering your time to work at a school function or a local community or nonprofit event. After helping out a few times, you should be able to raise your hand to lead end-to-end planning and execution of an entire event. This will provide a good foundation to begin your interviewing for an entry-level position with a major company.

In the Final Analysis

Event marketing is a very specialized career but one that's dynamic and exciting. The opportunity to move into other areas of marketing is limited, so think hard before committing to this path.

DEMAND GENERATION MARKETING

Of course, the objective of every marketing role is to create demand for a product or service. But the term *demand generation* is used to describe a distinct approach to marketing communication that plans and executes data-driven programs to acquire new customers and retain existing ones.

B2C and B2B industries use the demand generation model to market products (and services) not sold at retail outlets that generally require a more considered purchase. This means that the potential customer must gather and consider a significant amount of information about the product before making a purchase, for example, a company investing in office productivity software or someone considering changing his car insurance.

Many different titles are used to describe demand generation roles: acquisition marketing, database marketing, lead nurturing, e-CRM, loyalty marketing, marketing automation. But we focus on lead generation and customer relationship management because these two activities form the essence of this discipline no matter what the title. We also review the digital cousin of demand generation, inbound marketing, because this career path is rapidly developing.

Referring back to the marketing funnel, demand generation works at the middle and bottom stages. Lead generation finds qualified prospects and nurtures these interested "hand raisers" to a closed sale, that is, a customer acquisition.

Customer relationship marketing aims to keep that acquired customer a happy and loyal one forever.

Internet- and database-related technologies have revolutionized this field; consequently, digital skills are in great demand. The following section discusses the positions of lead generation and customer relationship marketing. These areas are where the action is today in marketing. So if you have solid quantitative skills, strong project management abilities, and a keen interest in data, these are terrific careers to consider.

Lead Generation Marketing Manager

(Related Titles: Demand Generation, Performance Marketing, and Conversion Optimization)

All those credit card offers you constantly receive is lead generation in practice in the financial services industry. That free consultation to lower your car insurance? That's also lead generation. If you have received these offers, it's because you were selected (targeted) to be marketed to via extensive data analysis. You were then sent a specific offer based on your profile: your age, address, income, past purchases. If you replied to the offer, you have now become a sales lead.

> You probably wonder if anyone really responds to these offers. Yes, they do. It's big business, and the lead generation marketing manager makes it happen.

A lead is simply a potential buyer who has expressed some interest in a company's products or services. Lead generation

111

describes the marketing activities used by companies to identify, nurture, and convert this prospect to a sale.

The lead generation marketer's job is to:
- Find prospective buyers via targeted media (direct mail, telesales, direct response ads, digital channels)
- Engage them with marketing communication (a brochure, a special offer)
- Get their contact information (name, company, title, e-mail address) through various offers (a free consultation, an industry white paper)
- Pass this contact information to the sales force so they can close the final sale
- Support the sales rep by continuing to deliver useful marketing communications to the prospective buyer

The lead generation manager relentlessly measures, analyzes, and optimizes program performance toward the goal of delivering the most qualified leads to sales in the most efficient way. Of course, the sales force will ultimately take credit for the final sale. But the lead generation marketer plays the key assist role.

Typical Job Description:
Lead Generation Marketing Manager

Formal Job Description	What This _REALLY_ Means
Develop the lead generation strategy to drive new customer acquisitions.	No business can survive without constantly acquiring new customers. Your work is

	essential to company growth and profitability.
Develop the customer segmentation strategy utilizing customer data, analytics, and lead scoring to identify high-growth customer segments.	Lead generation uses data to "fire a rifle with a precision scope," not a shotgun. You will need to eat, breathe, and sleep data to sharply define and segment your target customer!
Develop the marketing communication campaign. Create and execute campaign tactics, including direct mail, telemarketing, search marketing, digital advertising, blogs, events, website landing pages, and contact forms.	You can use any tactic you can think of—just drive leads within the available budget.
Design and execute testing and optimization programs, including A/B and multivariate testing programs to optimize conversion rates.	You are on a relentless quest to find the perfect marketing mix. It will be up to you to find the right mix of tactics that delivers the most qualified leads within your budget.
Create a lead scoring strategy to ensure that the sales force has the most qualified leads.	If you waste the time of a sales rep with bogus sales leads, she will not be happy!
Ensure data integrity, including database cleanliness and quality, and ensure the security of customer data.	A database is only as good as the accuracy of the information within. Most important, customer data is sacrosanct and can in no way be compromised.

CUSTOMER RELATIONSHIP MARKETING

The term *customer relationship marketing* is used broadly to describe a number of different jobs in sales, customer support, and marketing. This section defines CRM as a marketing activity that plans and executes data-driven marketing campaigns to create and maintain customer loyalty.

> Modern-day customer relationship marketing (CRM) was introduced in 1993 by the brilliant and wonderful Martha Rogers, along with her partner Don Peppers, via the concept of one-to-one marketing. This inspiring model discarded the outdated concept of database marketing and replaced it with a personalized approach to managing a long-term customer relationship.

CRM is based on the (accurate) theory that only a handful of customers accounts for the vast majority of a brand's profits. These most valuable customers (MVCs) are truly worth their weight in gold and form the foundation of CRM. The following questions best frame the key questions addressed by the customer relationship marketing manager:

- How does a company know who its MVCs are?
- How can data be used to provide better value to the customer?
- How can you keep them loyal and prevent their switching to a competitor?
- How do you convert a low spending customer to a high-value one?

The field of CRM has developed tremendously and is currently seeing its most rapid growth fueled by major advancements in database- and digital-related technologies. Companies are investing billions in marketing automation platforms, such as Salesforce.com, Adobe, and Marketo. These platforms serve several purposes, but they are all grounded in highly sophisticated databases of customer records. (A *record* means all information associated with the customer, including his contact information, demographics (age, income, education), and complete sales history). The strategic application of customer data has indeed become the heart of the marketing profession.

Customer Relationship Marketing Manager

(Also Called Loyalty Marketing, Database Marketing, Retention Marketing)
The CRM manager first develops the segmentation strategy based on analysis of customer data. He identifies which customers have similar demographic, psychographic, or buying profiles and groups these into customer segments. He then creates customized marketing communication and offers that best connect with each specific segment. For example, one customer segment could be defined as "suburban new parents"; another could be defined as "urban empty nesters." The CRM manager at a travel company, for example, would certainly send different vacation offers to these very different customer segments.

CRM skills and capabilities are in high demand across almost all industries and clearly represent a very smart career option.

Typical Job Description:
Customer Relationship Marketing Manager

Formal Job Description	What This _REALLY_ Means
Lead strategic planning to drive customer loyalty and retention objectives.	You will be running a business within a business and define your own programs and budget. Your strategy will be based on customer insights and data and will need to stand out in a very crowded and competitive field.
Segment the customer base and develop the customer contact strategy across each segment.	You must be fluent in the principles of customer segmentation. Defining segments, such as "working moms," enables the marketer to customize programs to appeal to similar consumer lifestyles and interests.
Work with the analytics team to identify and target high-value or at-risk customers.	Some loyal customers are more valuable than others are. Data insights will enable you to prioritize where you focus your time and program investments.
Plan and execute personalized and integrated loyalty marketing campaigns, including e-mail, direct mail, mobile, and digital channels.	You will need to constantly assess the cost against the impact of each channel you plan to use and find that combination of tactics that delivers the most bang for the buck. Sometimes the most basic channels, such as e-mail, drive the best ROI.
Partner with the analytics and insights team to collect and analyze data to develop customer insights to inform strategic	Ultimately, the quality of your strategic plan will be determined by the quality of your customer insights. Your analytics partner is your BFF.

planning.	
Lead external agencies to plan and execute highly creative and measurable customer relationship marketing campaigns.	The creative (artwork, copy, video) for your campaigns is done by an ad agency that usually works for multiple clients. You need to get more than your fair share of its time and attention to deliver great work. This is your second BFF.
Define, pilot, and rapidly iterate test-and-learn programs enabling campaign performance and ROI to be optimized.	Relentless testing and optimization is the bedrock of customer relationship marketing. Your program can always perform better; thus your work is never ever finished.
Build and maintain a state-of-the-art centralized customer database and related technologies.	You don't need to be a tech-geek but you do need to have a deep understanding of data-based related technologies.

What You Need to Be Successful

Superior = mastery / Strong = much better than average / Solid = competitive

The insightful management and application of data is a critical success factor for any demand generation career. The demand gen marketer must know how to acquire, structure, interpret, and apply customer data to deliver a customized marketing communication presentation—one that motivates the customer to respond and that ultimately delivers sales.

As with all marketing positions, a passion for getting inside the head of the customer separates the solid from the superior demand gen marketers. Data are important pieces of the customer puzzle. True insight and thus competitive advantage combines these quantitative insights with a more qualitative sense of customer needs, habits, ambitions, fears, and motivations. This combination delivers the highly targeted and personalized customer experience that maximizes response and ROI.

Skills Required
- Superior analytical thinking
- Strong strategic thinking
- Strong project management
- Strong written and oral communication
- Strong knowledge of marketing strategy, digital marketing, and marketing automation
- Strong knowledge of consumer privacy governance and database hygiene

Competencies Required
- Superior customer orientation
- Strong collaborative relationship-building skills
- Solid leadership skills
- Solid influencing skills

Pros	Cons
👍 Your impact on the business is quantifiable, albeit indirectly. 👍 A great field for data junkies. 👍 Very good career	👎 This field provides only limited exposure to other core elements of marketing, such as product innovation, pricing, and advertising. 👎 The work environment can be very demanding and results now

progression prospects.	driven.
👍 Relatively stable employment.	👎 Some CEOs and CMOs don't get data driven marketing and still value the TV ad marketing model of the last century.
👍 The pay can be very good.	
👍 You'll work with leading-edge marketing technologies.	
👍 The field is emerging as the primary marketing function in certain industries, primarily B2B.	

Career Path for the Demand Generation Marketing Manager

Career paths within demand generation take many turns, depending on the industry or company. In certain industries, such as financial services, lead generation and customer relationship marketing are central to the marketing function. Thus demand generation roles can evolve from manager (managing lead generation or CRM programs for a single brand) to director (managing multiple brands) to marketing VP or even chief marketing officer. Note that within other industries such as FMCG, demand generation is a secondary element of the marketing mix and does not offer a clear path to career progression.

Salaries

Lead generation and CRM managers can expect to earn between $80k and $120k plus a 25% to 30% bonus.

A Day in the Life of the Demand Generation Marketing Manager

8:30: Meet with product marketing to review latest product offerings

10:00: Review this week's results from the lead management campaign; identify areas for immediate campaign optimization

12:00: Lunch with new marketing technology vendor

13:00: Present loyalty marketing recommendation to senior management

14:00: Review final draft of customer segmentation report before sending to the boss

15:00: Finalize proposal to improve the quality of the customer database system

16:00: Review results of A/B testing program for new landing page design

17:00: Scan competitor websites to view new programs and tactics

Landing Your First Job

Several entry-level jobs can prepare you for a career in demand generation. Depending on the company, marketing analyst, database analyst, and customer service rep entry-level positions can serve as entry ways. As you search for your first job, it will be essential to highlight your quantitative and analytical skills. Any position that involves data analytics, especially related to sales or marketing campaign performance, will provide a solid foundation.

Any familiarity with the leading marketing automation platforms—such as Salesforce.com, Marketo, Pardot, Adobe, and HubSpot—will also position you well for an entry-level role. Consider investing in a marketing automation training course offered by HubSpot or another vendor. Most of these are free, the training is comprehensive, and you should receive a certification that can be added to your résumé. This certification does indeed matter because these are the platforms of the future, and the pool of experienced professionals is still quite low.

As you interview for demand generation jobs, be prepared to describe how you became a lead or member of a loyalty marketing program. What tactics did the brand use to influence you? Have they ever sold you on a more expensive product (the latest iPhone perhaps?) or influenced you to buy a complementary product (iPhone case, earbuds)? What did the brand have to do to earn you loyalty? Thoughtful answers to these kinds of questions should impress any potential hiring manager.

In the Final Analysis

If you thrive on data, analysis, and relentless optimization, then demand generation provides a high-paying and highly in-demand career option. A smart choice indeed.

Related Careers in Demand Generation

Inbound Marketing

Marketing automation platforms, such as HubSpot and Marketo, have led to development of the inbound marketing concept. While the principles of demand generation remain the same, inbound marketing is fully grounded in online marketing and works under the (valid) assumption that prospective customers are continuously online searching for, researching, and finally buying products. While traditional lead generation is about reaching out (outbound) to prospective buyers with various programs, inbound marketing is about creating programs that enable sales prospects to find you online, driving them *inbound* to your website and converting them to customers.

Inbound marketing requires expert management of search marketing, website content, web conversion, and e-mail marketing to drive web leads and sales. A simple four-stage process is used to explain the work of the inbound marketer:

1. *Find*: In the find stage, a variety of digital tactics—such as digital advertising, social media, search engine optimization (SEO), and search engine marketing (SEM)—are used to find potential customers who are online and actively researching a product purchase. The objective is simple, intercept their web browsing and motivate them to visit your website.

2. *Engage*: This stage is about presenting the website visitor with useful, informative, and engaging content about your product offering.

3. *Convert*: This stage focuses on driving the website visitor to immediately purchase your product or to acquire her contact information (most likely an e-mail address) so she can be marketed to ("nurtured") in the future.

4. *Retain*: The final stage is about continuing to manage the relationship with the customer and to stimulate future purchases.

Note: The find–engage–convert–retain framework follows the same logic as the marketing funnel, it's just tailored to the digital environment. Find and engage equates to the top of the marketing funnel (awareness and consideration). Convert equates to the middle of the marketing funnel (trial and acquisition). Retain equates to the bottom of the funnel (loyalty).

DIGITAL MARKETING COMMUNICATIONS

The digital marketing landscape is vast. In this section, we address only a fraction of the specialized career opportunities available. It's also important to note that every career option previously discussed in this book includes at least some aspect of digital marketing. So this section focuses on careers that are exclusively grounded in the digital world: website management, search marketing, social media management, and digital marketing management.

Finding a common definition for *digital marketing* is a challenge. One person may define digital as display (banner) advertising; another might consider website development as digital; yet still another would consider e-commerce as digital. But think of digital marketing as the integrated planning, execution, and measurement of all digital communication channels. It's about coordinating the full spectrum of digital subspecialties so they work together to achieve the marketing goals.

So as we review career options we will distinguish between the "orchestra conductor" who brings it all together (the digital marketing manager) and the "musicians in the orchestra" (search marketing, website communication, and social media).

Digital Marketing Manager

The digital marketing manager leads the integrated planning, execution, and measurement of a suite of digital communication channels. While the digital marketing manager need not be an absolute expert in any specific digital subspecialty, he does need expertise in:

- Understanding the customer's digital habits, attitudes, and behaviors
- Understanding the brand's overall marketing objectives and strategies
- Creating digital marketing strategies that perfectly align the above

The digital marketing manager supports the brand manager's or product manager's overall marketing program. Digital will play a specific role in this program, such as growing brand awareness among the Internet audience or driving trial through online promotions. Based on the objective at hand, the digital marketing manager writes the digital marketing plan specifying the target audience, digital tactics, budget, and campaign calendar.

The digital program consists of a complete set of activities, including SEO, SEM, website, e-mail, and social media. The manager selects each of these based on his knowledge of the customer's online behaviors, for example, which social media or search terms the customer uses or the type of smartphone the customer has. He also needs to design how the various digital components work together:

- What web content is necessary based on the search program?
- How should the brand's website experience complement the social media program?
- How should mobile complement the desktop experience?

The intent is to create an integrated plan that gets the digital tactics to work synergistically to efficiently achieve the marketing goals.

Ultimately, the digital marketing manager brings this all together into an integrated campaign calendar and leads its execution. Sometimes the manager executes each of the tactics by herself. Other times she uses the services of an agency or contractor for this.

Job profiles for digital marketing manager vary widely based on the industry. The following reviews a typical digital marketing manager role within a business-to-consumer company.

Typical Job Description: Digital Marketing Manager

Formal Job Description	What This _REALLY_ Means
Develop integrated digital marketing campaigns that support overall brand marketing objectives.	The digital universe is connected and so must your digital programs. Digital channels have unique attributes that achieve different goals. Your job is to align this Rubik's Cube for maximum impact.
Lead the development of digital tactics, including owned (website, e-mail, mobile), earned (social media), and paid (display ads, Google AdWords) media.	You need to consider any and all digital tactics and how they work synergistically. You don't need to be an expert in any one of them, but you need to be able to properly direct a team of

	specialists in search, website, social, mobile and e-mail marketing.
Establish measurement objectives for the overall digital campaign and key performance indicators for digital tactics, including search marketing, website visitor and engagement, and e-mail response rates.	With the exception of e-commerce, most digital marketing program results cannot be directly attributed to sales. You will need to select those metrics that matter most and measure them.
Lead in-depth market research to hunderstand consumer digital behaviors to inform the appropriate digital communication strategy.	You will need data and insights to think like your customer. Knowing how to ask a handful of the most important questions is the key to success here.
Be a thought leader in emerging media channels, vendors, tools, technology, and best practices. Identify and activate next-generation digital pilot programs.	There is only one person in the company who will be turned to for the guidance needed to remain relevant in the fast-moving digital space —that would be you!
Use A/B and multivariate testing to inform ongoing and relentless optimization of search marketing, website, social, and all other digital programs.	This sounds more complicated than it really is. You'll simply test whether your customers clicked more or less on certain components of your program versus others. Did they click more often on offer A or on offer B? Did the video or the photo on the web page get more interest? You keep learning what works best and continually update your program.

What You Need to Be Successful

Superior = mastery / Strong = much better than average / Solid = competitive

All digital marketing managers have a deep understanding of Digital 1.0 (web, search, e-mail) and Digital 2.0 (social and mobile) and related technologies. But the superior ones have a keen understanding of both traditional (offline) and digital marketing communication. They choose among a suite of digital channels, not based on if they're new and trendy, but if they can add value to and complement the overall marketing program in the most effective and cost-efficient way.

Critical to success is the digital marketing manager's collaboration with a wide variety of people. Superior managers work side by side with their brand or product marketing colleagues and are seen as invaluable team members. They can take highly technical digital jargon and simply and clearly communicate this to senior management. And they can work effectively with a cast of characters, including techies, creative types, and data geeks to create the overall digital experience.

Skills Required
- Superior knowledge of digital media and related technologies
- Strong strategic thinking
- Strong analytical thinking
- Strong project management
- Solid business planning and analytical aptitude
- Solid understanding of traditional marketing communications
- Solid written and oral communication skills

Competencies Required

- Superior ability to manage change
- Strong customer orientation
- Strong collaborative relationship-building capabilities
- Solid influencing skills
- Solid abilities as a creative problem solver

Pros	Cons
👍 It's the future of marketing!	👎 Less-than-progressive companies can still consider digital a secondary component of the marketing mix.
👍 Interesting and dynamic work where you are always growing as a professional.	👎 Job can be highly stressful at times.
👍 The job combines strategic, creative, and tech.	👎 There are frequently long hours.
👍 You work with very different and highly talented people.	👎 Digital budgets still lag behind traditional marketing budgets.
👍 Significant career progression potential.	
👍 Excellent experience for many career paths.	
👍 The impact of your work is measurable.	
👍 Good pay (and getting better).	

Career Path for the Digital Marketing Manager

Digital marketing managers have two career paths to choose from. One path is to stay specialized in digital and climb the ladder to digital marketing director and perhaps to vice president of digital marketing. The other path is to first specialize in digital and then move into mainstream brand or product marketing roles.

In my opinion, the latter is the smarter option because deep digital experience is essential in 21st century marketing. There is an old guard in marketing that currently occupies the coveted senior roles. Most of them are not making the digital transition, providing you with your opportunity to progress to marketing director, VP, and, ultimately, chief marketing officer.

Salaries

Digital marketing managers can expect to earn $80k to $130k plus a 25% to 30% bonus.

A Day in the Life of the Digital Marketing Manager

8:30: Review new website design & navigation options
10:00: Present next quarter's digital marketing campaign plan to the marketing VP
11:00: Meet with vendor to review new e-mail marketing platform opportunity
12:00: Lunch with Google AdWords sales representative
13:00: Review A/B testing plans for new campaign landing pages

> 15:00: Analyze results of recent content enhancements on SEO ranking
> 16:00: Finalize the digital marketing metrics dashboard for this quarter
> 17:00: Meet with market research to discuss web visitor research options

Landing Your First Job

There are normally two routes to digital marketing management, each requiring different levels of digital experience.

You can make the move into digital without deep experience by moving laterally within your current company. Any sales, marketing, or analytics experience is a solid foundation. But the great thing about digital is that we are all daily practitioners. Demonstrating your passion for and command of social, website, and mobile channels can indeed make you a legitimate candidate for an entry-level digital role. You will have a lot to learn, but digital is not all about technology. Having a solid business mind, knowing how to plan and execute programs, and working well with others are just as important. Digital opportunities should be expanding within your company—so raise your hand!

The other route is to seek an entry-level job at either an ad agency or a client-side company. This approach requires your demonstrating some level of experience in digital marketing. This could be experience you gained in working on a website for a local business, your school, or a nonprofit. As mentioned in the Demand Generation section, consider getting a certification in one of the leading inbound (marketing automation) platforms. This training is free, does not take too long, and focuses on the bread and butter of digital marketing.

> HubSpot (http://academy.hubspot.com/certificat ion-overview) says people with certification get six times more views to their LinkedIn profile pages.

In the Final Analysis

The digital marketing manager of today will be the chief marketing officer of tomorrow. Digital continues to reshape each of the 4 Ps of marketing. In the near future, *digital marketing* will simply mean "marketing."

See Appendix 1 for a list of great companies to begin your career with.

SEARCH ENGINE MARKETING

There are approximately 1 billion websites in the world and more than 3 billion web searches per day. Within this vast digital universe, brands compete every day for the attention of prospective buyers. Search engine marketing management is both the art and the science of influencing search engine page rankings enabling your brand or company to be listed ahead of competitors on the most popular search engines—namely Google, Bing. and Yahoo.

There are two subspecializations in search engine marketing management:

1. *Search engine marketing (SEM)*: Also known as *paid search* and *sponsored search*, SEM focuses on planning and executing paid search advertisements that appear above or alongside search results.
2. *Search engine optimization (SEO)*: Also known as *organic search* or *natural search*, SEO focuses on improving the ranking of a web page within the free search results that appear on the search results page.

Both SEM and SEO have the same goals: to deliver top ranking in search queries and to influence the customer to click on the ad or text link and visit a brand's or a company's web page.

The difference is that SEO delivers the above result for free, whereas the marketer must pay for these results with SEM. The obvious question is: Why pay when you can get the same result for free? The answer lies in the absolute necessity of getting your brand or company listed on the very first page of search results. More than 90% of search clicks are from the first page displayed by the search engine. This means that people browsing the web have very little patience to scroll through multiple pages of search results. So if you are not on page 1, you will probably be invisible.

> As the saying goes: "Where is the best place to bury a dead body? ... On the second page of Google."

Search Engine Marketing Manager

The search engine marketing manager is responsible for developing and implementing paid search marketing campaigns on the leading search engines to drive prospective buyers to the brand's website. In this role, the manager is responsible for getting search ads displayed in front of the right audience and then motivating them to click on these ads.

The SEM manager develops a keyword strategy that defines a long list of the words and phrases that a prospective customer might enter into a search engine. The manager then creates the copy for the ads displayed in the paid search results. Most important, the search engine marketing manager establishes the bidding criteria for each of these keywords.

Search engines, such as Google, get paid based on auction-like bidding for specific keywords. The greater the market demand by brands for a keyword, the higher the bid required to get your ad preferred placement in the search results. Bid too little, and you don't get good ad placement; bid too much, and you will run out of money and not make your site traffic goals.

The search engine marketing manager needs to continually measure and evaluate consumer responsiveness to the ads considering:

- Which keywords are driving the most website traffic?
- Which keywords are driving the most traffic for the least cost-per-click?
- What was the click-through rate (the number of times the ad was clicked on divided by the total number of times it was displayed)?
- Which ads are delivering the most sales conversion on the website?
- Are desktop or mobile devices searches generating the most web traffic?

This is a sought-after role and critical to the success of many small and large companies. If you are highly competitive, love data, and have relentless passion for continuous improvement, then search marketing could be a great career option.

Typical Job Description:
Search Engine Marketing Manager

Formal Job Description	What This _REALLY_ Means
Plan and execute paid search initiatives in support of overall brand or company marketing objectives, including national and geo-targeted campaigns in the leading search engines.	This is an essential role that can make or break a business. You are in the hot seat to deliver customers to the website 365, 24/7.
Create the SEM campaign and supporting tactics, including the	Success is completely based on sweating the details. There is _a_

keyword and bidding strategies.	*lot* of number crunching in this job, and it's critical to the success of the business!
Work collaboratively with the website manager and copywriters to plan and develop SEM-optimized landing pages.	The person who clicks on your search ad can't get confused when she visits your website. You need to work side by side with your web manager and others to create a seamless search-to-website experience.
Set up, schedule, and implement national and local geotargeted campaigns in key primary (Google, Yahoo!, and MSN) and secondary search engines.	This sounds complicated but it really isn't. You just don't want to try to sell snow shovels in Miami!
Relentlessly monitor, analyze and optimize bids to achieve the best possible ROI.	This is the essence of search engine marketing —getting clicks that matter but not spending a penny more than you need to.

What You Need to Be Successful

Superior = mastery / Strong = much better than average / Solid = competitive

Superior search engine marketers are relentless optimizers. They think like a shopper and consider what keywords best align to the prospective customer's purchase-decision journey:

- What might someone type into the Google search bar when he is in the early stages of considering a new television purchase?

- What might a person search for when he is now ready to purchase it?
- And how can the search engine marketer divert traffic away from a competitor's website?

Of course, strong search engine marketers love getting deep into the data and are never, ever satisfied. They are always striving for the perfect campaign—that program that drives lots of website traffic at the lowest possible cost.

Skills Required
- Superior knowledge of leading SEM programs, including Google AdWords and Bing
- Superior analytical skills
- Strong project management
- Solid oral, written, and interpersonal communication skills

Competencies Required
- Solid influencing skills
- Strong interpersonal and collaboration capabilities
- Solid and intuitive grasp of digital media and related technologies

Search Engine Optimization Manager

(Also called SEO Specialist, SEO Coordinator, SEO Strategist)
The search engine optimization manager is an important, albeit back-office, role in most organizations. One part content manager and another part technical, the SEO manager's job is to drive website traffic for free, that is, without buying paid search ads. She is responsible for ensuring that a website

indexes (ranks) as high as possible in search engine organic (free) search listings.

Search engines use sophisticated algorithms to interpret the search queries (or keywords) entered into the search box. These algorithms have only one goal: to deliver (index) a list of the most accurate and unbiased web pages that will best satisfy the search request. The SEO manager works hard to decipher this complicated and ever-changing algorithm but places particular focus on managing three components:

1. *Content*: The SEO manager ensures that the content on a website is written in an SEO-friendly manner. Thus he needs to make sure that the content on each web page takes into account the most likely keywords that could trigger a search for the information on that page.
2. *Tagging*: This refers to placing appropriate code on web pages that inform a search engine what information exists on there.
3. *Backlinks*: Backlinks refers to getting content on other websites to reference your brand's website and to include a live link (URL) back to your site.

The SEO manager also manages many other factors, but the above tasks are the ones that occupy the majority of effort.

Typical Job Description:
Search Engine Optimization Manager

Formal Job Description	What This *REALLY* Means
Develop the search engine optimization strategy based	Although this is a highly specialized role, you must be fully

on a comprehensive assessment of overall marketing goals, competition, and the industry.	informed by and aligned to the marketing teams.
Lead SEO campaigns from conception to implementation, including internal approval processes, account structure, keyword list development, and copy creation and testing.	There are SEO hacks and SEO professionals. This is a true discipline to managing this properly.
Establish SEO targets, monitor results, and report on a regular basis.	Your scoreboard is your SEO ranking. This is posted online every day for everyone to see.
Develop detailed keyword and linking strategies for optimal SEO performance.	This is the "secret sauce" of SEO strategy. You must think like the shopper to succeed.
Work closely with the website manager and SEM manager to inform web content and to coordinate fully integrated search campaigns.	The SEM and website manager rely heavily on your expert guidance to succeed in their roles.
Be the thought leader in search optimization trends and best practices ensuring leading-edge understanding of the latest enhancements to search engine algorithms.	*No one* fully understands the Google search algorithm, but you need to keep relentlessly trying.

What You Need to Be Successful

Superior = mastery / Strong = much better than average / Solid = competitive

SEO managers must think like a shopper and understand what (key) words and phrases they will enter into a search engine to guide their online shopping. He then ensures that these words and phrases are included in the content of his web pages. This maximizes the chance that the pages are indexed highly by the search engine and thus receive top listing in free search results. Superior SEO managers do this better than all their competitors do and are successful because they are relentlessly optimizing—there is no goal line in SEO.

Skills Required
- Superior knowledge of SEO across the leading search engines, including Google, Bing, MSN, and Yahoo!
- Strong data analytics skills
- Solid strategic thinking capabilities
- Solid knowledge of HTML, Google analytics, and webmaster tools
- Strong experience with SEO tools, such as SEOMoz
- Strong project management skills
- Solid oral and written communication skills

Competencies Required
- Solid interpersonal skills
- Solid ability to work collaboratively
- Solid influencing skills
- Strong ability to multitask and manage multiple priorities

Pros	Cons
🖐 SEO is a dynamic, ever-changing field.	🖐 It's a very specialized role that can be considered behind the scenes.
🖐 The work is highly quantifiable.	🖐 Good but not great pay.
🖐 You work with smart people across the organization.	🖐 Many factors impact search rankings that are out of your control.
🖐 Provides a solid foundation in digital marketing and future career development.	
🖐 Good job security.	
🖐 Strong potential to work as an independent consultant.	

Career Path for the Search Marketing Manager

Search marketing is an essential ingredient in the marketing mix of companies whose survival depends on finding and converting customers online. SEM skills are in great demand now and will certainly be well into the future. So search engine marketing can be a lucrative career path on the client side, in an ad agency, or as an independent contractor. Also, if you have ambitions to move up within client-side companies, an SEM background will serve as a great foundation for moving into a digital marketing manager role.

SEO careers are perhaps the most specialized in marketing. In most client-side companies, search engine optimization is considered more of a back-office-type role and would not be a good platform for future career growth. However, you have significant potential to develop your career with ad agencies and search consulting firms or as an independent consultant.

Salaries

SEM managers can expect to earn $60k to $100k plus a 25% to 30% bonus. SEO managers can expect to earn $50k to $80k.

Landing Your First Job

The bad news is that landing your first job will require experience in search marketing. The good news is that the leading search engines provide extensive and free training to learn SEM.

Through Google, you can immediately begin your SEM training with its AdWords Certification program (https://support.google.com/partners/answer/3154326?hl=en). Here you will find complete instructions and extensive online study guides. You will need to pass the AdWords fundamental exam as well as one of five other exams (search advertising, display advertising, mobile advertising, video advertising, or shopping advertising). Google offers no certification for SEO, but many resources are available both by Google and through search engine platform vendors and community forums.

For those interested in pursuing a search marketing career, I suggest getting certified by Google and then to get as much desk training as possible. Get some hands-on experience actually managing SEO or SEM for a website. It is likely that many small business owners or nonprofit groups would jump at the chance to have someone apply their knowledge to improve their site traffic. Some volunteer experiences would go a long way to opening doors for a full-time role.

In the Final Analysis

Search marketing offers a good-paying and stable career option. But think hard if you want to focus on such a specialized role.

WEBSITE COMMUNICATION MANAGEMENT

Delivering a great website experience is a hugely challenging yet ultimately rewarding
career option. Your work helps millions of people find useful information that better informs and guides them to a smarter purchase decision. It helps them troubleshoot or fix a product. And it informs them about your company. You are not just promoting; you are publishing. There are vast opportunities for both strategic and creative fulfillment in web communication management.

Of course, everyone in the company has an opinion about your website—and so they should. The website is the digital storefront of your brand or company and first impressions matter—*a lot.* A second-rate website radiates a second-rate company to every visitor. The website speaks volumes about the company's image, and if this is not reflected on the website, there is a big disconnect.

> What does it say about your company if a customer struggles to find the basic information she's looking for on your website? Or if the content she finds is incomplete or poorly written?

Many specialized positions are required to build and operate a world-class website: user experience, web design, information architecture, content strategy, front-end development, analytics, back-end development. Similar to the instruments in a great symphonic orchestra, each contributes a critical and indispensable element to the final piece. Web communication management plays the role of the conductor determining the music that will be played and leading all the players toward creating a work of both art and utility.

Website Communication Manager

(Also Called Web Communication Manager, Web Experience Manager)

The website serves as the central hub of the digital marketing mix, and all roads (digital ads, e-mail, social media, search) lead here to influence customer purchase through a satisfying and compelling experience. The website communication manager is responsible for the overall planning and implementing of this experience.

The brand website serves two masters, the site visitor (your customer or prospective customer) and the brand. A website that serves as nothing more than a digital version of your advertising provides little value to visitors—and they will immediately exit your site. On the other hand, a website that wonderfully educates or entertains visitors without selling is a poor investment. The website manager sits at the intersection of these two (not incompatible) objectives.

Your work as a website communication manager involves managing the day-to-day publishing of content (a new product launch, the latest sale or promotion, corporate news) while at the same plan planning new upgrades to the site experience. These could include a new site design; adding new functionality, such as an interactive game; integrating social media; or adding audio-visual tools.

About every three years, you will likely be leading a major upgrade of the entire website. Why every three years? Because the site you launched a few years back now looks outdated compared to the latest generation of websites. To do this, you will define site requirements—this means gathering a list of new enhancements that better meet the needs of marketing. Perhaps marketing now is seeking to grow its e-mail database and needs the website to collect consumer contact information. Or maybe the brand is now using video as an important part of its communication mix, so the site will need functionality to deliver this. You'll combine these requirements with your understanding of the latest web technology and the needs of your site visitors to create a web experience that delights your customers and influences sales.

Typical Job Description: Website Communication Manager

Formal Job Description	What This _REALLY_ Means
Develop the overall website strategy aligning site visitor needs with marketing objectives.	A great website serves two masters, the site visitor and the brand. You need to resolve the tension between these two priorities.
Define requirements for creating the optimal site user experience, including website design, information architecture strategy, content, and functionality.	Truly great websites are a rare thing and require aligning a complex mix of components to deliver a superior experience. This is the essence of web communication.

Lead the editorial planning and publishing of web content through the web content management system.	It's long been said that "content is king." You must approach web content as if you were a publisher, not an advertiser.
Define, measure, and report website key performance indicators, including user satisfaction, content engagement and site conversion.	You will have reams of data based on the clicks of your site visitors—but only a handful really matters. Your job will be to find these and act upon them.
Partner with the IT organization to define next-generation website platform enhancements enabling the website to remain best in class.	Web platforms require significant investments to remain contemporary. You will need to have a strong grasp of emerging technologies and assess which ones best support your website objectives.
Manage brand presentation across the website ensuring a premium and consistent experience globally.	Great websites fully reflect the character and integrity of the overall brand image across every single page. You will need to ensure this happens on your website.
Be a thought leader in digital, and provide recommendations to consistently drive website innovation.	Today's website will be obsolete within three years. You must stay on top of web design, user experience, and technology. And make sure your website remains ahead of the pack.

What You Need to Be Successful

Web communication managers possess a wide array of skills and competencies. The job requires both strategic thinking and strong executional skills. It requires strong design and creative instincts and a knack for technology and analytics. The web manager must also think like the customer and like a businessperson. He needs to manage today's real-time experience on the website while planning years into the future. Web communication managers are indeed a special breed.

Skills Required
- Superior understanding of digital marketing, web user experience, and technologies
- Strong project management
- Solid analytical thinking
- Solid written and oral communication skills

Competencies Required
- Strong collaborative relationship-building capabilities
- Strong customer orientation
- Strong forward-thinking capabilities
- Solid ability to motivate and influence others

Pros	Cons
👍 It's both a strategic and a creative position. 👍 You work with leading-edge digital	👎 It's a specialized role focusing on just one component of digital marketing. 👎 Good but not great pay.

149

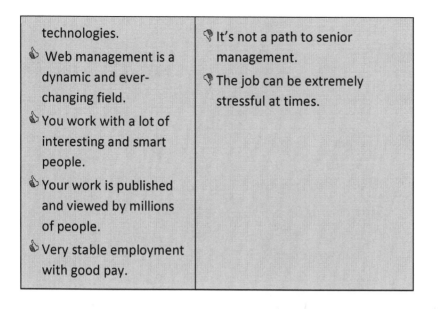

technologies.	👍 It's not a path to senior
👍 Web management is a dynamic and ever-changing field.	management.
👍 You work with a lot of interesting and smart people.	👎 The job can be extremely stressful at times.
👍 Your work is published and viewed by millions of people.	
👍 Very stable employment with good pay.	

Career Path for the Website Communication Manager

Website management is a highly specialized career and is not a path to senior marketing management. That said, it offers excellent opportunity to grow as a professional. You will be at the forefront of digital technology that is transforming virtually every industry. You will work with a lot of smart people with varied backgrounds and see every day (along with millions of other people) the results of your work.

Your experience as a web manager will ground you in many of the strategic, technical, and creative requirements of 21st-century marketing. Moving laterally into a digital marketing manager position is a likely avenue for further career progression. You will also have the opportunity to work in agency or consulting roles. Websites are here forever, and these skills will remain in high demand.

Salaries

Web communication manager salaries vary greatly, ranging between $50k and $120k plus a 15% to 30% bonus.

A Day in the Life of the Website Communication Manager

8:30: Check latest web content and application updates made to website

10:00: Meet with editorial team to plan content for holiday promotion

11:00: Review new home page design options with ad agency

12:00: Lunch with information technology director; discuss new mobile website

13:00: Debrief from brand team on new product launch and website   requirements

14:00: Review site visitor satisfaction survey results; discuss optimization plans

15:00: Conduct final review of new landing pages and push live to website

16:00: Attend Marketing Technology Trends webinar

17:00: Work on long-term strategic plan for website enhancements

---

Landing Your First Job

There is no defined entry way, but many paths can lead to a career in website management. Since virtually all digital specialties intersect with the website, experience in search marketing, content development, website analytics, and social media provide solid foundations.

There are many ways to gain basic website development skills. Simply creating your own website on any topic you are passionate about is a great first step. Also, there are many small businesses and nonprofit organization that would jump at the chance to have you design and build them a website. Platforms such as Shopify (http://www.shopify.com) and HubSpot (http://www.hubspot.com) have excellent, easy, and (relatively) low-cost ready-made platforms that require no software coding experience.

In the Final Analysis
Web communication offers a dynamic and stable career opportunity. You will never run the company, but you will be master of your own domain (pun intended).

Web (Digital) Content Manager
Web content management delivers the words, images, and graphics that are published on a website. However, this role can also be responsible for managing content across multiple digital channels, such as e-mail, blogs, and social media. The scope of the job can vary greatly—sometimes actually authoring the content, sometimes simply publishing content written by others. All positions generally include a level of technical skills with respect to using a content management system (CMS), the technology platform used to post web content.

Job Scope

As the saying goes, "Content is king," and a website cannot be great without great content. Great content is comprehensive but concise, factual yet entertaining, and serves the information needs of the visitor. The content manager may write all, some, or none of the content. Often the content manager hires and directs a team of freelance writers and copyeditors. Perhaps a better term for the web content manager would be digital editor or digital publisher since this is the real value of the role. Similar to a newspaper or a magazine, someone needs to plan and publish multiple streams of content but coordinate this in a way that delivers an overall editorial voice.

Skills and Competencies Required

A successful content management career requires superior writing skills and knowledge of editorial planning and storytelling across various digital formats, including web pages, blogs, and e-mail. Exceptional organizational skills and the ability to multitask and work productively in a deadline-driven environment are also essential. As far as technical skills are concerned, content managers need experience working with content management systems, as well as basic graphic design applications, such as Adobe Photoshop.

Career Path for the Web (Digital) Content Manager

Most companies view web content management as a highly specialized profession but one with ample opportunity to grow professionally. Entry-level positions have responsibility for a narrow range of editorial content. Within two to three years, you will likely manage a team of content creators (employees as well as freelancers) across several streams of editorial.

But a great content manager is usually a great writer, which is a highly prized skill across almost any field. A web content manager with strategic and quantitative capabilities would be a key candidate to advance in web communication and/or digital marketing management thus providing a career path with upward mobility.

Salaries

Content managers can expect to earn $60k to $100k plus a 15% to 10% bonus.

Landing Your First Job

There is no defined entry way, but indeed there are many paths to a career in web content management. A degree in English, journalism, technical writing, or a related field is an excellent foundation, as is some experience blogging and using a web-content-management system. Any proof points you can show to highlight your writing or editorial capabilities would also be very helpful. Gaining experience with content management systems requires some training, but the learning curve is not that steep. So get hands-on and create a website about one of your passions, write a blog, or find a sponsor who needs its website content refreshed. This will enable you to begin building out your portfolio to impress prospective employers.

SOCIAL MEDIA MANAGEMENT

Social media is the most transformative and complex communication medium in history. It brings us together as global citizens while at the same time isolating us in our own private Idaho of cyberspace. It can foster the widespread and immediate distribution of important knowledge but is mainly used to share rather inane personal information. It can instantly fuel a peaceful revolution or be used for public shaming and bullying. These contradictions aside, social media is truly the next frontier for marketers. Marketers who get this new medium will receive great benefits; those who don't will pay an enormous price.

Of course, social media is not just a single media platform like TV and radio. Rather, it is comprised of many different platforms with unique capabilities and characteristics. From a marketing standpoint social media can be segmented as follows:

- *Blogs*: Huffington Post, TMZ
- *Social networks*: Facebook, LinkedIn, Google+
- *Content sharing platforms*: YouTube, Pinterest, Instagram, Snapchat, Vine
- *Microblogs*: Twitter
- *Content aggregation platforms*: Mashable, Tumblr

Thankfully, these amazing properties were not first built to accommodate marketers and advertisers. They were built to serve a greater purpose and add unique value to the life of the user. Their application as a marketing platform came after the fact. As such, you will find social media properties that are thriving as marketing platforms while others are struggling.

Social Media as a Marketing Platform

Fundamentally, marketers need to ask themselves: How can social media uniquely help drive my sales? The world does not need another medium to deliver a simple ad impression or a coupon. So what does social media uniquely bring to the marketing party?

There are two fundamental benefits:
1. *Word-of-mouth marketing*: the most potent of all forms of marketing whereby your legion of loyal customers recommend your brand to their social network
2. *Highly targeted advertising*: whereby ads are displayed based on analysis of a person's unique social media profile and interests

When using traditional media, the marketer asks: What message do I want to deliver to my target audience? Good marketers *do not* approach social media in the same manner. Rather, the first question is: What content can I provide to my brand fans that they would find of value and want to share with their social network?

There are fundamental differences between these two questions and there is a new rule book for social media marketing that's grounded in fresh, progressive thinking. As you consider companies to work for, pressure test which rule book they are using.

Career opportunities on the client side of marketing include social media manager and social media community manager roles. The social media manager is the architect of the overall social media strategy and leads its execution and measurement. The social media community manager is the voice of the brand (or company) and directs the global conversation across all social channels. Despite being highly specialized, these jobs offer excellent opportunity for professional development—and under certain circumstances, excellent career progression.

Social Media Manager

The social media manager directs the activities of all social media channels to achieve specific marketing goals. The manager's social media strategy could focus at the top of the marketing funnel to help establish awareness of a new product introduction. It could work at the middle of the funnel, serving to generate sales leads. And finally, it could work at the bottom of the funnel to foster brand loyalty. Depending on the objectives, the social media manager creates a strategy that targets a specific audience segment, identifies which social channels to use, what content should be developed for each channel, and how to measure and optimize program performance.

With the strategy established, the social media manager directs the overall execution of the program. This could involve starting up an entirely new social media property (a new YouTube channel, for example) or creating programs for existing ones. Some social channels are visually driven—for example, Pinterest—and require the development of lots of photo and video content. Others are editorial drive content—

for example, Twitter and blogging—requiring extensive written content. No matter which channel, the social media manager ensures that the content developed speaks to the intended target audience in a meaningful way and that it stays focused on the defined marketing objectives.

> Responsibility for managing social media advertising such as Facebook ads, is sometimes the responsibility of the social media manager and sometimes that of the advertising manager.

Social media programs require a lot of administrative work, and there are many social media platforms (Spriklr, Salesforce, Studio, Spredfast, to name a few) that help brands distribute content and measure program results. An important responsibility of the social media manager is to choose the right platform, given the scope and complexity of its program.

Social media managers also monitor social channels to gather market and customer insights. The manager selects the social listening platform, such as the Salesforce.com Social Studio, and designs a program to continuously monitor the social buzz related to the brand, the company, competitors, or the industry. These insights are extremely valuable since they are real time and help the manager understand what the world is saying about his brand across the social media universe. With these insights, the manager then can create future social media marketing programs that connect with the customer at a more meaningful level.

Typical Job Description:
Social Media Manager

Formal Job Description	What This _REALLY_ Means
Develop the social media objectives, strategy, and marketing campaign.	Social media marketing is no longer an experiment; it's a profession. There is a rigor and discipline that you will be expected to apply.
Define key performance indicators for each social media channel and measure their success based on the brand's overall marketing.	Social media must be focused on achieving specific marketing goals. It's not about posting fun stuff and seeing what happens next.
Create and maintain social media channels, including Facebook, Twitter, Google+, Pinterest, Snapchat, Instagram, and Vine.	Social media channels continue to proliferate. Some will matter more to the business than others. You will need to figure out which ones do and do not.
Lead the social media agency to conceive and create content that is highly shareable and appropriate for specific channels.	In larger companies, you will likely have support from an ad or social media agency to create the programs and content. You will need to motivate them to get the best possible work out of them.
Implement the brand social listening program and make recommendations to improve the overall marketing program based on social buzz.	Social media provides a gold mine of customers' insights—their passions, issues, fears, and hopes. This can provide a brand or company with great information to inform product innovation and to improve marketing communication.

Serve as the thought leader for future social media trends and technologies.	Social media continues to spawn new platforms and technologies. Your job will be to figure which ones can help your business—before the competition does!

What You Need to Be Successful

Superior = mastery / Strong = much better than average / Solid = competitive

As you would expect, social media managers are masters of all things social. They use a half dozen or more different social platforms every day across all their digital devices. But the superior managers think strategically about how to apply the unique characteristics of each platform to achieve marketing goals:

- What's the role of Twitter versus Facebook versus Instagram from a marketing communication standpoint?
- Which channels reach the most members of my target audience?
- How should the social media marketing programs be tailored for each channel?

Successful social media managers are also deeply in tune with their audience and pour over hundreds of posts on any given day. These managers are often the most knowledgeable people in the company about consumer trends, competitive activities, and the reputation of the brand. A superior social media manager imparts this valuable knowledge to marketing, sales, product development, and the legal department to inform a better company. They are important people in the organization!

Skills Required

- Superior knowledge of major and emerging social media channels, including Facebook, Twitter, Instagram, Pinterest, Snapchat, Google+, LinkedIn, Vine, and YouTube
- Superior written and oral communication
- Strong project management
- Solid analytical abilities
- Solid digital marketing and marketing knowledge

Competencies Required

- Superior customer orientation
- Strong ability to build collaborative relationships
- Solid influencing skills

Pros	Cons
👍 Your work is in real time and seen by thousands (or millions) of people.	👎 It's a very specialized role that can be considered behind the scenes.
👍 Social media marketing is a dynamic industry that is constantly being reinvented.	👎 Salaries are good but on the lower end of the marketing pay scale.
👍 Your work is published and viewed by millions of people.	👎 It's not a path to senior management.
👍 It's real-time marketing that is constantly shifting based on social conversations.	👎 The job can be very stressful at times.
👍 Every day opens new opportunities and challenges.	👎 Often requires irregular working hours, including evenings and weekends.
👍 You work with very young and	

talented people. 👆 Excellent employment opportunities long term.	

Career Path for the Social Media Management

Social media is growing by leaps and bounds as a marketing platform and provides excellent career growth potential. That said, it is a highly specialized field. On the client side, social media would, at best, provide a midmanager-level career opportunity. Thus a community manager could be promoted to social media manager (managing programs for one or two brands) and could then be promoted to social media director overseeing all social media activity within the company.

On the agency side, social media would certainly be a career path to higher levels of management. You can also work for yourself as an independent consultant once you get the right level of expertise. Companies are increasingly dropping the staff-laden agency model, choosing to hire the specific skills they need at a fraction of the price. This fraction of a price still pays the independent consultant handsomely.

Salaries

Social media manager salaries vary widely and range between $50k and $100k plus a 10% to 20% bonus. Community manager salaries are typically less and pay between $35k and $70k.

A Day in the Life of the Social Media Manager

8:30: Scan customer posts across the brand's social channels

9:00: Meet with social community manager. Update Facebook editorial calendar

10:00: Review new YouTube channel design options with ad agency

11:00: Write a summary of last month's social media performance results

12:00: Lunch at desk; conduct midday scan of customer social media posts

13:00: Debrief from brand team on new product launch and social media goals

14:00: Review Facebook advertising campaign with ad agency

15:30: Review new social listening platform with vendor

16:30: Conference call to review new Google+ functionality

17:00: Final day's scan of customer social media posts

Landing Your First Job

Several years ago your intuitive knowledge of Facebook and Twitter, combined with some solid writing skills, could land you your first job. Today there are more expectations by employers for hands-on experience. Similar to the guidance provided for web communication, getting *any* relevant experience—at your school, a local business, or a not-for-profit group—will go a long way. Note that your prospective hiring manager may or may not have a clue about social media. So you will indeed impress her with your fluent understanding of Snapchat, Tumblr, and Vine. But as you interview, help her understand missed opportunities—how you can help her use these new channels to drive deeper consideration of the company's brand or activate social word-of-mouth marketing. The company needs you. It just needs to know why!

In the Final Analysis

It's a very specialized role, but a career in social media management will keep you at the forefront of the digital transformation.

Social Media Community Manager

The social media community manager is responsible for managing the conversation across one or more social media channels. This includes viewing, posting, and responding to brand or company comments across Facebook, Twitter, Pinterest, and all platforms. This role has swiftly become an essential component of brand communication.

As discussed in the Demand Generation section, only a handful of most valuable customers (MVCs) accounts for the overwhelming majority of a brand's sales and profits. In social media language, these are called *brand fans*. The role of the community manager is to be on the front lines of maintaining and nurturing relationships with this community.

The community manager's work strongly influences consumer perceptions of the brand, arguably even more so than advertising does. A great community manager speaks within the character of the brand or company but does so in way that connects with the audience in a genuine and personal manner.

The best community managers are honest, responsive, and always positive no matter what the situation. This takes a very talented person.

Typical Responsibilities: Social Media Community Manager

The community manager works with the social media manager to develop and manage the editorial calendar for a brand's (or a company's) social media channels. She also collaborates to plan, source, and create content, including text, photo, video, and infographics. On a daily basis, the community manager posts this content and finds opportunities to engage in real-time conversations with the brand's fans.

An important role of the community manager is to redirect customer inquiries to other people within the organization; for example, a product complaint would be sent to customer service, a job inquiry sent to the HR department. The community manager is also responsible for reporting any social conversations that could have legal, security, or brand reputation risks. (There are some crazy people out there with a lot of time on their hands to rant and rave!)

Skills and Competencies Required

Outstanding writing and verbal communication skills are essential, as is an intuitive sense of the language and culture of social conversations. Deep knowledge of digital media and current and emerging social media channels is obviously critical, and the community manager must be able to simultaneously manage multiple priorities.

Related Careers in Digital Marketing

E-mail Marketing Manager

You will likely see postings for "e-mail marketing" as you conduct your job search, but consider this is an outdated term. Refer to the Demand Generation/Customer Relationship Management section of the book since this is where e-mail marketing is applied in a strategic manner—maintaining and nurturing customer relationships. There are companies that simply send out e-mail spam and hope for the best. But you don't want to work for any of these outfits because your learning and career advancement prospects will be extremely limited.

Content Marketing

Content marketing is a relatively new job title but based on the age-old concept of the advertorial. Whereas traditional marketing buys media to deliver the brand message via advertising, advertorial marketing delivers information that the consumer finds of value, for example, helpful household tips or how to better manage your family finances. In this model, the brand does not deliver an ad message but benefits from positive association it receives by providing the consumer with information of value.

Digital and social media have taken this concept to an entirely new level called *content marketing*. Content marketing distributes value-added information across various digital and social channels toward the goal of driving a higher level of engagement with the consumer. The content marketing manager takes direction from the marketing team to define program objectives—lead generation? Web visitors? He then hires and leads a team of writers, art directors, and designers to create content for multiple digital and non-digital channels.

The content manager 'creates once for distribution to many'. This means that he first thinks through all the media channels that are part of the marketing plan and coordinates production of all content formats at the same time. For example, the content manager will coordinate a single video shoot to capture all the footage necessary for a 10-minute video that might appear in YouTube, as well as a 30-second video that might appear on the website. This saves time and money while ensuring that all creative maintains a similar style.

This is a job that requires a multidimensional skill set, including editorial planning, writing, and design skills across various media formats: video, web, mobile, and print. Most important, the best content marketers are creative storytellers.

Interaction Design and User Experience

Interaction design and user experience (UX) are fascinating and growing specialties. Both focus on optimizing the way consumers experience digital devices, websites, and the pages within them. I have always struggled to gain a clear understanding of the difference between the two, but here's my best crack at it.

Interaction design is about creating a language between a digital property and its user:

- Where does the customer begin her website browsing on the screen?
- How does she interactive with the video player?
- Once the user has made an online purchase, how does she check out?

The interaction designer plans exactly how users interact online and then designs the digital interactions (buttons, drop down menus, sliders) and the right appearance (shapes, colors, sizes) to make it as easy as possible for the user to complete the purpose of their visit.

While interaction design focuses more on the micro-interactions, user experience focuses more on the overall end-to-end experience of the website visit. In the old days, computers were designed by engineers to simply achieve the essential business task. The last thing the engineer considered was the person (user) actually operating it. As the PC era evolved, the concept of user-centered design arose based on the (now obvious) notion that computers and websites should be designed based on how people naturally interact with them.

User experience design is a core component of any website design and works to define the overall site experience so the site visitor is a happy one from the moment she lands on the site to the moment she exits it. So UX optimizes the website design, how the pages are organized (the site map), and how the visitor moves from one web page or section to the next (navigation).

Careers in both interactive and user experience design require exceptional training. A number of private and university courses are available for a fee. I recommend Bentley University's User Experience certification course. This will provide you with excellent training (available online) and you will receive your credentials from a highly reputable leading university. Career prospects in this area are highly promising and salaries are quite good ($60k to $100k+), so it would likely be a smart investment.

Digital Graphic Designer

Digital graphics are the visual images and designs that appear on a web page. The digital graphic designer determines which graphics to use and how they are presented on a web page to create a beautiful and powerful experience.

We have all seen web pages so cluttered and disorganized that it's impossible to focus the eye. Great digital graphic designers know how to find the right balance of content and white space, making it easy to locate key information. They also know how to assemble photos, infographics, and video in a way that commands you to interact with them. The digital graphic designer plays a key role in getting site visitors to engage with the web page, a critical success factor if the consumer is going to be influenced by it.

Graphic designers can easily evolve their careers to such areas as interaction design and UX design or to a more senior digital creative manager position. The pay is so-so ($50k to $70k), but future growth potential is strong. You will obviously need some training or experience in art and design, as well as training in the leading digital publishing tools, such as Adobe InDesign, Illustrator, and Photoshop. But courses are readily available and usually require only a few days of training each.

Web Development Roles

Web development is not a marketing role, but as a digital marketer, you will depend heavily on these talented people to build and operate your website and applications. The following provides a basic understanding of the key types of web developers you may be interacting with.

Front-End Developer

The web is entirely virtual. Every web page and component of the page is made possible through lines and lines of code. Front-end development creates the code required to deliver what you see on a web page.

Go to any website using the Chrome browser and click "control U." Here you will see the work of the front-end developer created with HTML, CSS, JavaScript, and other programming languages. Front-end developers work closely with the interaction and UX designers and bring the web page concepts to (virtual) life.

Back-End Developer

The beautiful work of the web designer and front-end developer is simply a bunch of code sitting in a web server. A technology platform is required to store and deliver this code and other applications to the site visitor. Back-end developers build, connect, and operate the various technologies (web servers, application servers, databases) that enable this information to be accessed and served to the website visitor. They work in the world of .Net, Java, PHP, and MySQL, and run the engine room that makes this digital thing possible.

Mobile App Developer

Mobile app developers focus on the coding required to make what you experience on a smartphone. Similar to work on websites, mobile app developers work with interaction designers, information architects, and UX designers to bring these concepts to code. While there are many operating systems, the mobile app developer primarily works on the Android (used by Samsung smartphones) and iOS (used by Apple devices) platforms. Since almost every digital marketing plan now includes a mobile campaign experience, you will certainly be working with these talented people.

Information Architect

Websites can consist of tens of thousands of pages of information. Information architecture is the art and science of organizing this information to make it as effortless as possible for the site visitor to navigate the site and find exactly what she is looking for. Part of this role involves creating the site map, which specifies each of the various sections of the website, how each section is aligned to one another, and the exact order of web pages within each section. The information architect is also responsible for what's called *taxonomy*, which determines how to classify or label website content. This takes thoughtful planning and consideration of the end user's mindset and how she searches for information on the web.

Marketing Optimization

Marketing optimization is responsible for measuring, analyzing, and continually improving the performance of market campaigns—the relentless optimization of a brand's advertising, event, pricing, promotional, and digital program performance for maximum effectiveness and efficiency.

Because marketing campaigns are now heavily dominated by digital tactics, so too are marketing optimization roles. Consider a marketing analyst as someone who optimizes performance for campaigns that include both traditional and digital tactics, whereas a digital marketing analyst optimizes marketing campaigns that exclusively use digital media.

Marketing Analyst

Marketing analysts are responsible for measuring, analyzing, and recommending how to maximize the ROI of marketing campaigns that use both offline and online tactics. They work closely with the marketing strategy and execution teams to help them make smarter business decisions aided by data.

The marketing analyst first acquires a deep understanding of the marketing objectives and identifies how to define success of the program. Because there are so many variables that impact the sales of a product, leading marketers establish key performance indicators (KPIs). KPIs are measures that are highly correlated to sales and enable marketing programs to be held more accountable to their specific contribution to it.

Direct mail response rate, brand preference, and lead conversion are a few such examples of KPIs.

With the KPIs established, the marketing analyst puts in place the measurement system to track and capture these data. The marketing analyst then analyzes results against the established KPIs and creates a customized marketing dashboard. The marketing dashboard transforms reams of customer data and presents them in organized and visually impactful ways enabling the marketer to quickly grasp their meaning.

The marketing analyst works across offline and online media. Thus she measures and optimizes such tactics as direct mail, retail promotions, and consumer promotions, as well as digital ads and website and social media tactics. Most important, she looks across the full spectrum of tactics to identify the mix of tactics, creative, and offers that deliver the KPI goals in the most cost-efficient way.

Digital Marketing Analyst

Annual spending on digital ads, social media, and paid search is well over $100 billion dollars and continues to grow at double-digit rates. Digital is no longer just an experiment; it's a big investment, and marketers demand optimal returns on this investment. The digital marketing analytics manager delivers data-driven insights that enable the marketer to plan and execute finely tuned and high-performance digital campaigns.

The analyst begins by understanding the overall digital marketing objectives and structuring a measurement plan against these:

- How many web visitors should be expected based on the investment?
- What's the target for the digital advertising click-through rate?
- How many site visitors should we expect to convert to a sale?
- What's the e-mail open rate target based on historical benchmarks?

An essential role of the analyst is to recommend what metrics define a successful program – before the program is executed. The analyst then relentlessly measures and recommends ways to optimize these success metrics. They will interpret the click-stream behavior of consumers to assess which tactics most cost efficiently deliver the intended marketing objective— usually sales conversion. Each set of clicks (for example, clicking on a digital ad, search listing, or online video) provides important intelligence about the consumer's purchase behavior and thus a potential insight to sales conversion.

A major advantage of digital marketing is that results are available in real time, enabling winning and losing program features to be quickly identified. The digital marketing analyst uses A/B and multivariate testing to test different variables to optimize program performance.

- Which landing page design best drives sales conversion?
- Does Photo A or Photo B achieve the highest click-through rate?
- Which social media post is driving the most content sharing?

This relentless testing leads to continuous recommendations that enable the digital marketing manager to optimize ROI.

There is a host of measurement tools (Google Analytics, Omniture, and others) in the analyst's tool kit—one to measure social media, another for web visitors, and still others for mobile and e-mail marketing. The digital marketing analyst must be an expert in managing these tools to deliver accuracy and timely data.

Other responsibilities of the digital marketing analyst include developing custom marketing dashboards for campaign reporting and assessing the performance of offline channels—such as TV, outdoor, and newspapers—versus online channels.

Skills and Competencies Required

This career is simply about taking tons of information and converting it into actionable and timely insights. Digital marketing analysts and marketing analysts need exceptional analytical and project-management skills and must have a keen eye for detail. They also need to be able to communicate findings in a clear and convincing way to management, so solid writing and verbal communication skills are important.

Salaries

Marketing analysts and digital marketing analysts earn anywhere between $60k and $110k plus a 15% to 25% annual bonus.

In the Final Analysis

The dynamics of customer buying will never be completely understood, and marketers will perpetually be on the quest for the perfect marketing mix. Marketing and digital analytics provide well-paying and stable career opportunities for the (digitally) analytically minded individual interested in pioneering a new marketing science.

Related Careers In Marketing Optimization

Web Analytics Manager

Web analytics manager jobs typically exist in companies where the website is the primary digital channel. The objective of the role is to analyze where site visitors came from and what they did on the site to uncover better and more cost efficient ways to increase site traffic, engagement (what people view and click on), conversion (completing a sale or sales lead), and the overall satisfaction of the site visitor. This role is increasingly morphing into the more relevant digital marketing analyst one as companies expand their digital footprint.

Social Media Analyst

Social media is growing in size as well as complexity, and smart marketers want smart insights to optimize their results. The social media analyst is an emerging role that supports the social media manager to create customized measurement programs across all social channels, such as Facebook, Twitter, YouTube, Pinterest, and Vine.

The analyst collects and interprets this data and recommends ways the marketer can create more effective content within the brand's social communities. The analyst is also responsible for setting up and monitoring the social listening program to get to answer any one of a number of key questions such as:

- What programs are driving the most conversations?
- Which Facebook ads are getting the most clicks?
- What content is getting shared most by brand fans with their social networks?
- What are consumers saying around the world about the company or brand?
- What cultural trends are evident via social conversations?
- What language or slang might the marketer adapt to better connect with his audience via advertising?

For the most part, marketers are still rather confused when it comes to understanding the ROI of their social media investment. As the medium continues to gain an ever greater share of the marketing budget, this role will continue to develop as a solid career path.

Marketing Operations Management

Marketing operations develops and runs the technology infrastructure that optimizes marketing effectiveness and efficiency across the company. This role focuses primarily on managing the databases and reports that capture and analyze campaign performance. Ensuring that the marketing analysts and campaign managers in the company have fast and accurate access to these data is a source of competitive advantage and the key responsibility of the marketing operations manager. Marketing operations is also responsible for deploying technologies that makes the marketing teams more productive, such as project management and workflow software applications.

Technology is rapidly evolving and having a big impact on marketing measurement, and optimization and marketing operations is at the forefront of this. It's a behind-the-scenes role but an important one.

PART 3

THE INDUSTRY VIEW OF MARKETING

Marketing roles exist in all industries, including health care, consumer goods, information technology, and financial services, among many others. But the role and stature of marketing varies significantly by industry. So you need to reflect on a number of important questions as you consider which one provides the best career path for you.

Key Questions
- Is marketing the driver of the business, or is it simply considered a support function?
- What is the higher purpose of the business? Are its products and services truly valuable to people and helping to make the world a better place?
- How developed is the marketing function at the company? Will working there provide you with leading-edge marketing skills?
- Is the industry growing, or is it fading into the sunset?
- How big are the marketing budgets? Big bucks or a shoestring?
- Last but not least, what are you passionate about? What will keep you interested and motivated over the course of your career?

Following are some thoughts on several industries I have firsthand experience within.

Within **Fast-moving consumer goods** (FMCG) marketing rules the roost. This is a marketing-driven industry practicing the profession at its most sophisticated level. The success of any FMCG company depends heavily on the skills of the marketer. Of course, when you were a kid, you probably did not aspire to grow up to market toothpaste, and humanity is only marginally served by introducing the next new advancement in hair care. Also, consumer packaged goods companies typically compete in low-growth categories with intense competition. It's challenging enough just to maintain the current level of market share.

The **technology industry** is driven by engineering and sales with marketing playing a supporting role. But you will be working with fascinating products that are the engine of today's economic growth. While you will have limited influence on what products are sold, you will lead the other 3 Ps of the 4 Ps of marketing determining what channels to sell in, what the price should be, and how to promote. Marketing budgets are generally robust, and you'll gain experience with leading-edge lead generation and CRM marketing technologies. While marketing does not get the respect it does in FMCG companies, you will have an important role in driving the success of the business.

My **healthcare industry** experience is within medical devices, also an engineering and sales-driven industry. With the exception of pharmaceutical companies, marketing is rather underdeveloped as a profession and generally supports the activities of the sales force (sales events, trade brochures). Nominal budgets are allocated to marketing, and often the senior marketing roles are given to high-potential salespeople as career development opportunities. So your boss may not have any deep marketing experience—clearly, not a great way to first learn the trade. However, you will be working in an industry with an unmatched greater purpose: to improve health and save lives. I have also found that the people in this industry are the most sincere, respectful, and caring coworkers I have experienced.

Special Note about Digital Marketing

In many industries, digital already dominates the marketing mix; in others, it remains woefully underadopted. Often it's an old-fashioned mindset that limits adoption, despite overwhelming evidence of effectiveness and efficiency. During my time at IBM, the marketing department simply could not expand its thinking beyond traditional advertising. Astonishingly, the integrated marketing communications department did not consider the web, e-mail marketing, and search marketing its responsibility. While there were indeed several progressive thinkers and exceptions to this mindset, it all starts with the direction (or lack thereof) set by the CMO and other senior marketing executives.

I mention this because digital career opportunities are growing exponentially while the 20th-century TV ad model continues its slow but unmistakable decline. As you interview for jobs, it's important that you assess the digital mindset of potential employers. Pressure test the progressiveness of the people you meet with—are they 21st- or 20th-century marketers? Many great digital marketing opportunities are out there, and you want to align yourself only with companies that are looking to the future.

PART 4
FINAL THOUGHTS

Building off the last chapter, it's really important to think through many things as you point the compass for your first job in marketing. The more honest you are with yourself now, the more the compass points in the right direction, minimizing any rethinking about what you really want to do in the future.

Start by considering your passion and interests. Overlay on top of this your key strengths and differentiating talents. Factor in your tolerance for stress and scope of responsibilities. And then adjust for career growth and earnings potential. And presto! You have found the perfect marketing career.

If only it were that simple.

It takes a lot of deep thinking about many factors to make the right career choice. Hopefully, this book has provided you with some clarity about this vague thing called *marketing* and which career options might be best suited for you. My career has had its ups and downs, but there has certainly been much more good than bad. I'd do it all over again. So give it a good think, and keep me posted on your progress!

APPENDIX 1
GREAT COMPANIES TO BEGIN YOUR CAREER

Brand Management

Procter & Gamble http://us.pgcareers.com/
Unilever https://www.unilever.com/careers/
General Mills http://careers.generalmills.com/
Coca-Cola http://www.coca-colacompany.com/careers/
PepsiCo http://www.pepsicojobs.com/en
Mondelēz International
http://www.mondelezinternational.com/careers
Danone http://www.danone.com/en/for-
you/candidates/growing-in-danone/jobs-careers/
Heineken http://www.theheinekencompany.com/age-
gate?returnurl=%2Fcareers
L'Oréal http://www.loreal.com/careers/home-careers
Diageo http://www.diageo-careers.com/
Dean Foods
https://deanfoodscareers.hua.hrsmart.com/hr/ats/JobSearch/
index
Kimberly-Clark http://www.careersatkc.com/home.aspx
Kellogg's http://www.kelloggcareers.com/global/home.html
Johnson & Johnson http://www.careers.jnj.com/home
Anheuser-Busch http://www.buschjobs.com/

Estée Lauder Companies
http://www.elcompanies.com/Pages/Careers.aspx
Campbell Soup Company
http://careers.campbellsoupcompany.com/
Dole Food Company http://www.dole.com/en/about/careers
Avon Products http://www.avoncompany.com/careers/
Yum! Brands http://www.yum.com/careers/
The Clorox Company
https://www.thecloroxcompany.com/careers/
Mars, Incorporated
http://www.mars.com/global/careers.aspx
Kraft Heinz Company
http://www.kraftheinzcompany.com/careers.htm
The Hershey Company
https://www.thehersheycompany.com/careers.aspx
Colgate-Palmolive
https://jobs.colgate.com/?utm_source=careersite
ConAgra Foods http://www.conagrafoodscareers.com/

Product Marketing

Consumer Electronics
Samsung Electronics
http://www.samsung.com/us/aboutsamsung/
Sony
http://www.sony.com/en_us/SCA/careers/overview.html
General Electric http://www.ge.com/careers

Information Technology
IBM http://www-03.ibm.com/employment/
Intel http://www.intel.com/content/www/us/en/jobs/jobs-at-intel.html
Microsoft Corporation https://careers.microsoft.com/

Apple http://www.apple.com/jobs/us/
SAP https://www.sap.com/careers/index.html

Sport & Fitness
Nike, Inc. http://jobs.nike.com/

Telecommunications
AT&T http://att.jobs/careers

Healthcare
Boston Scientific http://www.bostonscientific.com/en-US/careers.html

Direct Marketing and E-Commerce
Financial Services
America Express https://careers.americanexpress.com/
Capital One Financial http://capitalonecareers.com/
Discover Financial http://www.mydiscovercareer.com/
State Farm Insurance https://www.statefarm.com/careers
GEICO Insurance http://careers.geico.com/
Allstate https://www.allstate.com/careers.aspx
Wells Fargo https://www.wellsfargo.com/about/careers/
Visa Inc. https://usa.visa.com/careers.html

Travel and Hospitality
Expedia, Inc. http://expediajobs.findly.com/
Priceline.com http://careers.priceline.com/

e-Retailers

Best Buy htt http://www.macysjobs.com/p://www.bestbuy-jobs.com/

Newegg http://www.newegg.com/Careers/

eBay https://careers.ebayinc.com/join-our-team/

Overstock.com http://www.overstock.com/careers

Macy's http://www.macysjobs.com/

IKEA http://www.ikea.com/ms/en_US/jobs/join_us/

The Home Depot https://careers.homedepot.com/

Gap

http://www.gapinc.com/content/gapinc/html/careers/gap-careers.html

Lowe's Home Improvement http://careers.lowes.com/

Toys "R" Us http://www.toysrusinc.com/careers/

Staples Inc. http://careers.staples.com/

Walgreens http://careers.walgreens.com/

Williams-Sonoma http://careers.williams-sonomainc.com/

Pottery Barn http://www.potterybarn.com/customer-service/employment.html

PetSmart https://careers.petsmart.com/

SHOP.COM http://www.shop.com/careers-v.xhtml

Amazon.com https://www.amazon.jobs/

Walmart http://careers.walmart.com/

Target Corporation https://corporate.target.com/careers

Media & Entertainment
Netflix https://jobs.netflix.com/

Barnes & Noble http://www.barnesandnoble.com/h/careers

Fashion
Zappos https://jobs.zappos.com/

Victoria's Secret https://www.victoriassecret.com/careers

L.L. Bean, Inc. https://llbeancareers.com/

SEPHORA   http://www.sephora.com/careers

J. Crew https://jobs.jcrew.com/

APPENDIX 2
MARKETING RESOURCES

Essential Marketing Reads

Ad Age: http://adage/com

Adweek: www.adweek.com

Marketing Management (Philip Kotler)

Ogilvy on Advertising (David Ogilvy)

Positioning: The Battle for the Mind (Jack Trout and Al Reis)

The 22 Immutable Laws of Marketing (Jack Trout and Al Reis)

The Global Brand CEO (Marc de Swaan Aarons)

Permission Marketing (Seth Godin)

Strategic Brand Management (Kevin Keller)

Tribes (Seth Godin)

The Long Tail (Chris Anderson)

Influence: The Psychology of Persuasion (Dr. Robert Cialdini)

Eating the Big Fish (Adam Morgan)

APPENDIX 3
MARKETING ASSOCIATION WEBSITES

American Marketing Association: http://www.ama.org

Association of National Advertisers: http://www.ana.net

Direct Marketing Association: http://www.the-dma.org

Mobile Marketing Association: http://www.mmaglobal.com

Internet Marketing Association: http://www.imanetwork.org

Marketing Research Association:
http://www.marketingresearch.org

Digital Analytics Association:
http://www.digitalanalyticsassociation.org

Digital Marketer: http://www.digitalmarketer.com

Business Marketing Association: http://www.marketing.org

APPENDIX 4
MARKETING JOB WEBSITES

LinkedIn: http://www.linkedin.com

Monster.com: http://www.monster.com

The Ladders: http://www.ladders.com

MarketingJobs.com: http://www.marketingjobs.com

Glassdoor.com: http://www.glassdoor.com

Indeed.com: http://www.indeed.com

CareerBuilder: http://www.careerbuilder.com

MediaBistro: http://www.mediabistro.com

Talentzoo: http://www.talentzoo.com

MarketingHire.com: http://www.marketinghire.com

Simply Hires: http://www.simplyhired.com

Marketing Edge: http://www.marketingedge.com

American Marketing Association: http://www.jobs.ama.org

Onward Searcher: www.onwardsearch.com

Made in the USA
Columbia, SC
17 January 2024

30586655R00107